Exam Grade Booster:
GCSE Spanish

Liam Porritt

Checked and approved by:	
Richard Lokier	Head of Spanish, Tonbridge School BA (Hons) in MML (French & Spanish), Downing College, University of Cambridge Examiner for an international exam board
John Witney	Head of Modern Languages, Westminster School BA in French & Spanish, MA in Language & Literature in Education, PhD, University of London PGCE (MFL), University of Cambridge
Cristina Cordero González	Examiner for an international exam board Spanish teacher & native speaker Licenciada en Filología Clásica, University of Seville
John McIntosh	Head of subject professional development programmes at United Learning Former Head of Spanish, Tonbridge School MA in Spanish & Theology, University of St Andrews
Lindsay McDonald	Head of Modern Languages, Tonbridge School MA in Modern Languages (French & German), St Edmund Hall, University of Oxford

Published by Exam Grade Booster
(Publisher prefix 978-0-9930429)
www.examgradebooster.co.uk

ISBN-13:   *978-0-9930429-1-1*

Disclaimer

The author and named checkers and approvers of this publication give no guarantee of improved examination performance nor will they be held responsible for any mistakes which may appear in this publication. They are not responsible if this publication, in any way, has a detrimental effect on its reader(s) or any other persons. This publication offers suggestions which have produced results for the author, but does not in any way state that these methods are the only ways of succeeding in GCSE or IGCSE examinations. All of the information given may not be entirely correct for all examination boards. The information given will not be inclusive of everything required for every examination board.

Credit

Special thanks go to Graham Samuels who must be credited with showing me the acronym 'CROATIANS', as used on pg. 46.

OTHER BOOKS BY THIS AUTHOR

Exam Grade Booster: GCSE French

Exam Grade Booster: GCSE German

Exam Grade Booster: IGCSE Chemistry Edexcel

The Rules of Revision

OTHER BOOKS IN THIS SERIES

Exam Grade Booster: GCSE English

Exam Grade Booster: IGCSE Biology Edexcel

Exam Grade Booster: IGCSE Physics Edexcel

Contents

About Us

About The Author

I have been extremely fortunate to attend one of the best schools in the country and in this book I aim to share the outstanding, exam-focused teaching which has led to my success. I believe my experience and knowledge of revising for and then taking GCSE and IGCSE examinations make this guide uniquely suited to preparing any student for success in their own Spanish exams.

It has taken me over two years to produce this guide having started it in the summer holiday following my GCSEs. My first guide, *Exam Grade Booster: GCSE French*, received extremely positive reviews. The Independent Schools' Modern Languages Association called the book 'a very worthwhile purchase: wholeheartedly recommended' while one Amazon reviewer writes that the book 'has helped [her] immensely and [her] results are improving, with [her] confidence doing the same'. Therefore, I decided to keep a very similar format in this book, with much of the same advice included while also ensuring that I incorporated plenty of Spanish-specific guidance too. I firmly believe that this guide will enable any student, willing to spend a little time and effort, to boost their grade and make the most of their potential. My goal is to share with everyone the techniques and tricks I have learnt while studying Spanish, particularly those which others can emulate in both the revision process and the exam room itself.

About The Checkers & Approvers

The checkers and approvers of this book are all qualified teaching professionals. Among them, there is a mix of native Spanish speakers and second language learners to ensure that content sounds like it is coming from a native, while maintaining a suitable difficulty for English students of (I)GCSE Spanish. They all share the author's goal of providing students in any schooling environment access to the same superb, exam-driven advice.

How to Use this Book

This book is designed to boost your Spanish GCSE or IGCSE grade. It is suitable for both UK and International qualifications for all examination boards.

The book has three sections:

- The first section is designed to outline exactly what is required in each of the four parts of your Spanish examination (writing, oral, reading and listening) in order for you to achieve better results.
- The second section will then target the areas of your Spanish exam which you can improve using my tried and tested methods. It is essentially a tool box of things you need to boost your grade.
- The final part will give you specific essential learning to do. It contains the information you absolutely must know as well as clever hints and tips to help you understand the tricky bits.

The first section should be read through as you would read any ordinary book from start to finish. The second and third sections do not have any particular order, so I would advise you to flick through and pick out the areas you feel will be most useful.

There are some sections which are only applicable for either GCSE or IGCSE students, so skip over any bits which are not relevant to you. They are clearly marked.

Section I

The Exam & What You Need To Do

Writing Examination

The writing examination is the **essay** component of the exam and will be marked according to the following three criteria:

1. **Communication**
2. **Use of language**
3. **Accuracy**

Communication

- Have you understood the assignment, and written appropriately (about the correct topic)?
- Do you respond to **all** the points of the assignment in your essay?
- Have you given opinions?
- Do you give justified reasons for the opinions given? E.g. why do you like or dislike something?
- Does your essay make sense?

If yes: you answer all the points clearly with reasons for why; and yes: the examiner can understand your essay, you will get **full marks** for this area.

So, how do you respond to all points of the assignment clearly?

Simple! All you have to do is write one paragraph for each point of the question. (I will explain more on this in a minute!)

The first and most crucial point about writing any essay in Spanish is to make sure you write what you know, and don't write what you don't know. Do not be afraid to make up the content of your essay! The story of your essay does not have to be factually correct. The examiner does not know you and does not care if you have really done what you claim to have done. The exam is a test of your knowledge of the Spanish language, not a test of how eventful your life has been. For example, if your daily routine involves waxing your legs (...boys!?), using a hairdryer and eating freshly picked guava, don't try to say all that because you don't know how to... And neither are you expected to! You can make up **anything** as long as it answers all the points of the essay.

So how do you answer all the points of the essay?

Standard GCSE (not IGCSE)

Depending on your task, you will be given two, three or four points to answer in your writing assignment(s), and these will test:

- Your use of tenses: the past, present and future
- Your vocabulary

For example, if your assignment were as follows:

A Spanish magazine wants you to write an article about your daily routine, giving details of what you did yesterday. Don't forget to include what you liked and what you disliked about each aspect of your routine. Also include how yesterday's routine may have been different from your normal schedule.

The article should also contain changes you would like to make to your daily routine in the future, with reasons for all of these adjustments.

In the above assignment, you can use the following tenses:

Tenses	To...
Preterite and Imperfect (Past)	Describe yesterday's routine as well as what you liked and disliked about it
Present	Say what you normally do and how yesterday's routine was different from that
Future and Conditional	Describe and justify changes you would like to make to your routine in the future

(For more information on the tenses above, go to pg. 81.) So, a minute ago I said that I would explain more on having one paragraph for each point of the question, and here it is: for the above assignment, to gain full marks for **Communication**, simply write three paragraphs of roughly equal length. The first paragraph should be about your routine yesterday as well as what you liked and disliked about it, the second about what you normally do compared with what you did yesterday, and the third should incorporate the changes you would like to make to your daily routine in the future. That's it.

IGCSE Only

You will be given four or five bullet points (in Spanish) to respond to for each essay title and each of these will give you an opportunity to demonstrate your use of the various tenses and your knowledge of vocabulary.

For example, if the question were as follows:

Hoy en día el calentamiento global es un asunto cada vez más emotivo. Por eso un periódico quiere obtener tu opinión sobre la situación. Deberías mencionar:

- *Lo que hiciste la semana pasada para proteger el medio ambiente*
- *Por qué elegiste adoptar estos métodos*
- *Tu opinión sobre si el calentamiento global es un problema serio o no*
- *Cuáles serán las consecuencias si no se reduce el calentamiento global*
- *Cómo los humanos combatirán el calentamiento global en el futuro*

Here, you could use the following tenses:

Tenses	To...
Preterite and Imperfect (Past)	Describe what you did last weekend to help the environment and why
Present	Give your opinion on the seriousness of global warming
Future and Conditional	Say what the consequences of global warming will be and how we will combat it

(If any of the tenses above are not familiar to you, or you simply want to understand more about them, turn to pg. 81.) So, a minute ago I said that I would explain more on having one paragraph for each point of the question, and here it is: for the above question, to gain full marks for **Communication**, simply write five paragraphs of roughly equal length with each one answering one bullet point. The first paragraph should be about what you did last week to help the environment, the second about why you chose to adopt these methods, and so on...That's it.

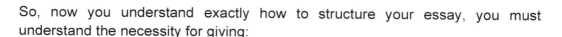

All Candidates

So, now you understand exactly how to structure your essay, you must understand the necessity for giving:

- Reasons why you did things
- Opinions of what you did
- Reasons for those opinions

If you want to get a high grade, this is not just important - it is **critical!** On every mark-scheme for every exam board there will be marks available for giving these three things, so make sure you give them all regularly throughout your essay. The Spanish words *porque* and *puesto que* meaning *because* should appear at regular intervals throughout your essay... If they don't, it means you are not justifying your actions or opinions enough.

Use of language

This mark is awarded according to how well you use Spanish. Do you know the basic and more complex tenses? Do you use fluid constructions, with justified opinions throughout your essay? Do you use long sentences with connecting words (such as *therefore*) to link ideas? (Don't worry; we'll come onto all this later.)

FIRSTLY, IT IS ESSENTIAL YOU USE A VARIETY OF TENSES THROUGHOUT YOUR ESSAY TO BOOST YOUR GRADE.

You should know the basic tenses (present, imperfect, preterite and future) and if you don't, learn them ASAP (they are in the *Specific Essential Learning* section from pg. 84-100). I know it's dull, but they are crucial. However, using set phrases, it is easy to spice up these tenses and you should already know some pretty simple but effective vocabulary which can be manipulated to form a good essay.

To boost your mark in this area, all you have to do is use your knowledge of tenses combined with set phrases. Use both 'standard' phrases and 'opinion' phrases in the correct places and use them to form long sentences which make sense – easy! (There is a list of both these types of phrase starting on pg. 35.) It is vital that you use both these types of phrase, as without opinion phrases you will not achieve a top grade – simple! Justifying why you do things throughout your essay is fundamental: always remember the three bullet points at the top of the previous page.

There is one more trick that will help to boost your **Use of language** mark: talking about other people. Throughout your essay you will spend most of the time talking about yourself, but to make it more interesting and to show off your grammar knowledge, try occasionally (maybe only twice) to mention someone else. For example, *Me gustaría trabajar cuando termine mis estudios pero mi novia tiene la intención de asistir a la universidad.*

Accuracy

This is simply how few mistakes you make.

This is the hardest aspect to improve, and relies on your spelling, the correct use of tenses and agreement. This will be covered as fully as possible in the *Specific Essential Learning* section and also on pg. 57, which takes you through how to check your essays for grammar errors. However, if you learn the set phrases, and use them correctly, you can guarantee that they will be 100% correct, in both their use of vocabulary and tenses. Therefore, these phrases will improve your mark for both **Use of language** and **Accuracy**. I shall come onto **Accuracy** in more depth later, but in general:

GOLDEN RULE :
WRITE WHAT YOU KNOW, DON'T WRITE WHAT YOU DON'T KNOW
Don't think of a sentence in English and then try to translate that into Spanish because you will make mistakes. Instead, think what you know (phrases and vocab) and fit that into your essay.

I also have two other Golden Rules for your writing exam:

> ## GOLDEN RULE :
> ## DON'T WRITE TOO MUCH
> When you are given a word limit, don't go over it by too much because this will only increase the number of mistakes you make, and you will gain NO CREDIT for writing more.

> ## GOLDEN RULE :
> ## USE PHRASES BUT DON'T FORCE THEM
> When writing an essay, include as many phrases as you can, within reason. However, do not force them into an essay if they do not make sense. This will lower your **Communication** mark as well as your **Use of language** mark.

So, there is more specific advice on your writing exam, including a list of brilliant phrases to boost your mark for **Use of language** and advice which will definitely improve your **Accuracy** starting on pg. 34.

However, I would recommend you keep reading this section to find out how to boost your marks in your oral, reading and listening examinations, before turning to the *Tools to Boost Your Grade* section.

Standard GCSE (not IGCSE)

The section on your *Controlled Assessments* (starting on pg. 19) will give you more information on the writing component of your exam.

Oral Examination

All Candidates

Rules

<u>Before the exam:</u>

- Prepare answers to questions (related to your task if you are doing standard GCSE or related to topics on your syllabus for IGCSE) before the oral exam. The best prepared students get the best marks. It is incredibly hard to come up with answers to questions spontaneously under the pressure of an exam. So, you must go through answers to questions before the exam itself. There is a list of virtually all possible questions for different topics on pg. 61.

- Prepare **opinions** and **reasons** for those opinions while you practise answering questions. Remember, justification is key.

- In this preparation, use the same techniques as demonstrated previously in the *Writing Examination* section, using both standard phrases and opinion phrases to boost your mark (starting on pg. 35).

- It is up to you how you prepare. You can either write down answers to the oral questions or simply mentally prepare them. However, it is essential that you repeat your answers over and over again speaking them to yourself (over the course of a few weeks) so that, when it comes to the real exam, you have answered questions similar to the ones you are being asked before and therefore know roughly what to say.

Tip: Use your phone or tablet to record yourself speaking answers and then listen to your responses. This way, you will hopefully be able to spot some of the mistakes you make. Furthermore, the act of listening to yourself speaking is proven to help you remember information. So, answering questions will become easier the more you:

- Practise answering possible questions
- Listen to yourself

If there are words you find particularly difficult to pronounce, ask your teacher if he/she would mind you recording himself/herself saying these words for you to listen to and then say yourself.

- Make this preparation part of your routine as you do not need to be sat at a desk to do it! You could do it each evening, or while you are in the shower, or walking to school – whenever suits you, but make sure you do it.

IGCSE Only

You will have to do a short presentation, followed by a couple of minutes of conversation based on the topic you have chosen for your presentation. There will then be 2 more conversations of roughly 3 minutes, each of them broadly about 1 of the following topic areas: Home & abroad; School & work life; House, home & daily routine; The modern world; Social activities, fitness & health. (There is a list of virtually every possible question for these exact topics starting on pg. 61.)

As said above, it is up to you how you choose to prepare. However, I would advise preparing a few things which you can use for virtually any topic area:

- A description of a film. Say what it is about and why you liked it. This can be used if asked: What did you do on holiday? (*I went to see a film called... It was about...*) What did you do last weekend? What do you do in your free time? What did you do for your birthday last year?

Tip: It is quite difficult to describe a film, so maybe look for a synopsis in Spanish online, go through it with your teacher so that you understand everything, and then edit it so that it is not too long and it is in your own words. Add in your opinion of the film and reasons why you liked or disliked it at the end. (I am not encouraging plagiarism - that is wrong - but finding something online and then editing it to be your own is fine!) For my Spanish oral, I used *El Laberinto del Fauno* (*Pan's Labyrinth*)... And notice I used the Spanish title for the film as opposed to the English one; this is far more impressive.

- A description of a book. Say what it is about and why you liked it. (For my Spanish oral, I described and gave my opinion of *El Hobbit*.)

 **All Candidates**

During the exam:

Sustain and expand on the answers you give. So, for example, the two following conversations are from two different candidates in their English oral:

Oral Conversation 1:
Examiner: "So, where do you normally go on holiday?"
Candidate 1: "I normally go to Spain."
Examiner: "Why do you go there?"
Candidate 1: "Because Spain is pretty and the weather is nice."
Examiner: "Where did you go last year?"
Candidate 1: "France."
Examiner: "Did you enjoy it?"
Candidate 1: "Yes."
Examiner: "So, where are you going to go next year?"
Candidate 1: "I am going to go to Spain with my family."
Examiner: "What are you going to do?"
Candidate 1: "Relax on the beach."
Examiner: "Anything else?"
Candidate 1: "Yeah, I'd like to read and would like to visit Barcelona."
Examiner: "Oh, how come?"
Candidate 1: "I'd love to see Gaudi's architecture."

Oral Conversation 2:
Examiner: "So, where do you normally go on holiday?"
Candidate 2: "I tend to go to Spain with my family because I think that it is very pretty and the weather is normally terrific. However, last year I decided to go to France with my friends and we had a great time because there were loads of things to do."
Examiner: "Where are you going to go next year?"
Candidate 2: "I am planning on going to Spain with my family, and I hope that the weather will be good because I would love to spend a week relaxing on the beach. I will spend lots of time reading and I will visit Barcelona because I've always dreamt of seeing Gaudi's architecture."

Which conversation is more impressive? Well, Oral Conversation 2 would definitely score far more marks than the first one, **BUT** both these candidates know virtually the same amount of English (ok, the second knows slightly more vocab and a few neat phrases, but not that much more). So, the key here is to speak as much as possible. The questions from the examiner are there to prompt you as to what to say, not to trick you. You can tell how well your exam is going by how much the examiner speaks: the less the examiner speaks the better.

However, stay on topic. For the holiday example above, don't start talking about your school because this will lose you marks for **Communication**.

The key is to be prepared but, during the exam, to sound like what you are saying is completely spontaneous and that you are simply making it up as you go along (when of course you are not). This can be done by:

- Throwing in a few *umms* and *ahhhs*, to make it seem as if you are not just recalling a prepared answer, but actually speaking. It is essential you sound spontaneous! Equally, it is important that you do not have too many long pauses in which you say nothing. Therefore, instead of sitting there *umming* and *ahhing* for ages when you are struggling to think of what to say, use words like ***pues*** and ***bueno*** (equivalent to saying *well...* in English) to give yourself time to think.
- Trying to change your intonation (not ridiculously) throughout your conversation so that you don't sound like your most boring teacher.
- Not being embarrassed to try and use a Spanish accent. There are marks on offer for your accent, and even if your accent is not brilliant, it is better than speaking Spanish in a plain English accent. The examiner will be happy just because you are giving it a go. On the contrary, when you can't be bothered to even make an attempt at an accent and sound like a lost English tourist in Magaluf looking for 'La Costa del Sol' what impression do you think that gives?... First impressions count, so at least try.

So, the Golden Rules for your oral exam:

> **GOLDEN RULE :**
> **SAY WHAT YOU KNOW, DON'T SAY WHAT YOU DON'T KNOW**

> **GOLDEN RULE :**
> **BE PREPARED BUT SOUND SPONTANEOUS**

> **GOLDEN RULE :**
> **EXPAND YOUR ANSWERS**

> **GOLDEN RULE :**
> **BREATHE SLOWLY AND REMEMBER: EVERYONE IS NERVOUS BEFORE THEIR ORAL!**

Standard GCSE (not IGCSE)

Controlled Assessments: Writing & Oral Exams

You are lucky in comparison with people doing IGCSE. You are allowed to:

- Find out the precise title(s) of your essay(s) and oral conversation before your exam
- Plan your essay(s) and your oral in preparation for your exam
- Use a dictionary

The first thing to say is that the precise details of what you will have to do both in preparation for your tasks and in the tasks themselves will vary depending on which exam board your school uses for Spanish GCSE. Most of you will have to write **two essays** and have **one oral conversation**. All three of these tasks need to be on **different topics**. The essays will each need to be around 250 words long. (However, you must confirm the exact details with your teacher.)

Writing

So, once you have found out the title(s) of your essay(s) (from now on I shall presume you will be writing two, but if not just adapt the system for one), you will need to stick to the following procedure in order to achieve the best possible marks.

| Find out essay titles | Write essays in own time | Produce plans and teacher feedback | Learn essays | Nail the exam! |

When writing your essays, you will be able to use:

- The material your teacher has given you on each of the topics covered in your two essays
- The material given in this book

This combination will help you to produce the best possible essays. They both need to be at the top end of the word limit, but remember not to go over it! All of the advice for the writing exam in the previous section applies here and is still crucial.

Once you have finished writing your essays, you need to produce a plan (the number of words allowed on this will depend on your exam board so ask your teacher) which you will be allowed to take into the exam room. Most exam boards also allow a few diagrams. It is up to you what you choose to write, but I would advise key words from each sentence which will prompt you what the rest of the sentence said along with a diagram which will remind you what each paragraph is about.

Note: Most exam boards will not allow you to include conjugated verbs in your plan, so you must put particular emphasis on learning exactly how the verbs you will be using in your essays (and your oral) conjugate.

For example, if one of my sentences were:

Me encanta ir al teatro con mi familia puesto que allí se me olvida el mundo real. - I love to go to the theatre with my family because, there, I forget the real world.

I would include the following words in my plan:

teatro, familia, olvidar

Once you have completed your two essays and your two plans, your teacher will check through your plans and it will be up to you to make sure you learn your essays thoroughly. Then, all you have to do is copy them out in the exam room from your memory (with your plans to help you) and you are sorted!

I know that this sounds like an awful lot of work, but it really does produce the results you are after. I cannot guarantee anything, but I managed to get 100% in my Italian GCSE after just 8 months of studying the language using this technique. Trust me, when you get that result, all of the hard work preparing is worth it!

The last point to make is on the use of dictionaries. At the start I said that being able to use a dictionary was lucky... It is, but only if you use it properly.

Dictionaries should only have **two** uses in the examination room:

1. To **check** the **spelling** of any words included in your prepared essay which you are not 100% sure of as you write it out.
2. Very occasionally if there is a word which you know was included in your essay in English, but which you can't quite remember in Spanish.

GOLDEN RULE :
DO NOT USE A DICTIONARY IN THE EXAM TO LOOK UP WORDS WHICH WERE NOT INCLUDED IN YOUR PREPARED ESSAY

If you have followed my system, there will be no need for this. Just remember the following Golden Rule when you are preparing your essays and when you are writing them out in the exam room:

GOLDEN RULE :
WRITE WHAT YOU KNOW, DON'T WRITE WHAT YOU DON'T KNOW

You will make sure you do this by using the information in your notes and in this book while writing your essays initially, only using a dictionary (can be online) to look up the occasional word.

Oral

The oral exam is in fact very similar to the writing exam. You will know the precise topic area of your oral conversation before the exam itself, so (using the questions on pg. 61 and any information your teacher may give you) you need to prepare answers to questions which you could possibly be asked. Once you have done this - either mentally or writing them down - you need to become familiar with your answers so that you can use parts of what you have prepared in the exam itself.

That's all there is to it really. All of the previous advice for both the oral and writing exams still applies when you are preparing for and taking your controlled assessments, so make sure you follow it!

Reading Examination

All Candidates

This about reading tell you boost at GCSE with easy steps. Don't worry; I know this is not good English (in fact there are 10 words missing). The point is that you don't need every detail to understand something. In your reading examination, you are **NOT** expected to understand every word. It is a test of your comprehension as well as your knowledge of Spanish, so **DO NOT PANIC!** Use the words you understand to work out what the passage is about, and use clues such as the title or the questions in response to the passage in order to deduce what is going on. Here is a sample passage, which could be a text from a Spanish GCSE Paper. There are no questions, but there are notes on how to establish what the article is about.

La salud mental de la gente que vive sola sufre
23 de enero de 2014

Según una investigación llevada a cabo en España, la gente que vive sola es propensa un 70% más a sufrir depresión que aquellos que viven en pareja.

El estudio analizó alrededor de 2,500 casos de depresión y los investigadores han enfatizado el hecho de que el número de familias encabezadas por una sola persona en los países desarrollados ha aumentado en los últimos veintiséis años. Hoy en día, una de cada cuatro personas en los Estados Unidos y el Reino Unido vive sin la compañía de otra.

Durante la investigación se habló con una pensionista, María, que vive cerca de Valencia, quien afirmó: "No me gusta nada vivir sola sin marido ni hijos en casa. Necesito encontrarme a menudo con otros miembros de mi familia o con mis amigas para conservar mi capacidad de conversación." Esta declaración reafirma claramente lo que muestran las estadísticas – sin otra gente en la vida el cerebro sufre.

Los científicos piensan que vivir solo puede estar asociado a sentimientos de aislamiento y a una falta de confianza, mientras que el viejo dicho: "Un problema compartido es un problema reducido a la mitad", parece ser cierto.

El estudio incluyó a 1127 hombres y 1373 mujeres (de 16 a 63 años) y en la investigación, a los participantes se les preguntó si vivían solos o con otras personas. Se les cuestionó también sobre las circunstancias de su entorno de trabajo, educación y condiciones de alojamiento, así como sobre sus hábitos de bebida, tabaco y ejercicio.

Los investigadores descubrieron que la gente que vivía sola consumió un 70% más de antidepresivos. En este momento no se hace mucho para mejorar la situación pero está clarísimo que deberíamos actuar inmediatamente para ayudar a estas personas que sufren.

Key Points to look for in Reading Exam Questions

Title

The title will give you an instant idea of what the article is about. Here, let's assume you don't know what 'salud' means*. We can still work out that the article is about: *The mental 'salud' of people who 'vive sola' suffers.* You should know that 'vive' is from the verb *vivir* meaning *to live*. Then, let's try and work out what 'sola' could mean. It is difficult to be sure, but we know that in English *solo* means *alone*, so let's go with *alone*. Therefore, from the title, we already know that the article is something to do with mental suffering and people living alone. (The title actually means: *The mental health of people who live alone is suffering*.)

* 'salud' means *health*

English Words

The highlighting on the next page shows all the words which we can work out purely from knowing English. From this alone, we can deduce most of what is being said in the passage. (If you didn't have a clue the first time you read it through, read it again once you have finished this page, paying close attention to the highlighting.) I would advise doing this in your exam: whilst you are reading through the passage, highlight or underline any words which are obvious to you from your knowledge of English, even if you haven't ever seen them before in Spanish.

Furthermore, use other languages you may study to help you work out what words mean if you do not recognize them. E.g. If you do French, *vivre* means *to live*... therefore, you can work out what *vive* (in the title of the passage) means in Spanish (*live*)!

Read Questions Then Text

Always read the questions **before you read the text** as these will give you a clue as to the content of the passage. They will also make you aware of the information you need to look out for when you are reading the text. (I know there are no questions for the text above... I am trying to show that even with a hard text and no questions you can still get the gist of it!)

La salud mental de la gente que vive sola sufre
23 de enero de 2014

Según una investigación llevada a cabo en España, la gente que vive sola es propensa un 70% más a sufrir depresión que aquellos que viven en pareja.

El estudio analizó alrededor de 2,500 casos de depresión y los investigadores han enfatizado el hecho de que el número de familias encabezadas por una sola persona en los países desarrollados ha aumentado en los últimos veintiséis años. Hoy en día, una de cada cuatro personas en los Estados Unidos y el Reino Unido vive sin la compañía de otra.

Durante la investigación se habló con una pensionista, María, que vive cerca de Valencia, quien afirmó: "No me gusta nada vivir sola sin marido ni hijos en casa. Necesito encontrarme a menudo con otros miembros de mi familia o con mis amigas para conservar mi capacidad de conversación." Esta declaración reafirma claramente lo que muestran las estadísticas – sin otra gente en la vida el cerebro sufre.

Los científicos piensan que vivir solo puede estar asociado a sentimientos de aislamiento y a una falta de confianza, mientras que el viejo dicho: "Un problema compartido es un problema reducido a la mitad", parece ser cierto.

El estudio incluyó a 1127 hombres y 1373 mujeres (de 16 a 63 años) y en la investigación, a los participantes se les preguntó si vivían solos o con otras personas. Se les cuestionó también sobre las circunstancias de su entorno de trabajo, educación y condiciones de alojamiento, así como sobre sus hábitos de bebida, tabaco y ejercicio.

Los investigadores descubrieron que la gente que vivía sola consumió un 70% más de antidepresivos. En este momento no se hace mucho para mejorar la situación pero está clarísimo que deberíamos actuar inmediatamente para ayudar a estas personas que sufren.

So, using what I have said, here is the general idea of each paragraph. You could work this out without me. (Honestly, I know the passage seems complicated, but when you spend time thinking about it and use the three key points on pg. 24, it's really not too bad!)

Paragraph 1: We can tell that there is an investigation in Spain and something about living alone being related to 70% more (people) suffering depression.

Paragraph 2: We can see that this study analysed 2,500 cases of depression and that the investigators 'somethinged' that the number of families with one person has increased (been *augmented* – from '*aumentado*') in the last years. In America and the United Kingdom, one in four people are without company (assuming you know what '*sin*' and '*una*' mean).

Paragraph 3: We are told something about the investigation and a pensioner named María from Valencia. We can tell that she is giving her opinion because of the speech marks and the word '*afirmó*' which evidently signals she is about to *affirm* something. She clearly doesn't like living alone (hopefully you know what '*no me gusta nada*' means!). She then speaks about needing (from '*necesito*') members of her family to conserve her ability (capacity) to hold a conversation. We are then told that her declaration reaffirms the statistics.

Paragraph 4: There is something about scientists and living alone being associated with sentiments (feelings) of lacking (from '*una falta de*') confidence. There is then an expression or quote about problems being reduced.

Paragraph 5: It is clear that the study included 1127 men and 1373 women aged 16 to 63 and that a distinction was made between living alone and living with other people. In the investigation, the participants were questioned (asked) about the circumstances of 'something', their education and the conditions of 'something', as well as about their habits relating to tobacco (clearly something about smoking) and exercise. We can deduce that the investigation examined the general wellbeing of people both living alone and with other people.

Paragraph 6: We see that the investigators found that 70% more antidepressants were consumed by people living alone. Then, there is something about the situation at the moment and acting immediately to help (from '*para ayudar*') the people who suffer.

Having understood all of this, you will definitely be in a very strong position to answer any questions. Just remember this golden rule:

> ## GOLDEN RULE :
> ## YOU WILL NOT UNDERSTAND EVERY WORD, BUT YOU DON'T NEED TO

So, up until now, this section has dealt with getting the gist of the hardest passages on the reading examination paper. However, you still have the task of answering the questions which accompany these passages. In all (I)GCSE examinations the majority of questions do not involve you writing in Spanish, but instead include box ticking, English responses and multiple choice style questions. Clearly to answer these questions, all you have to do is understand what both the passage and the questions mean.

Having said this, **examiners will try to trick you...**

...Therefore, there will always be a few questions in both the reading and listening papers designed to do just that. Examiners trick students by giving them two or more pieces of information related to a question, with the first piece of information either not the precise answer to the question or only a part of the information needed to get the right answer, so please be careful and look out for this!

There is an example of this in the text we just analysed (on pg. 25) where it says: '**una** de cada **cuatro** personas en los Estados Unidos y el Reino Unido vive sin la compañía de otra' (in the second paragraph). Here, it would not be uncommon for examiners to see the answers *una persona* and *cuatro personas* to the question of how many people live alone in the U.S.A. and the United Kingdom. First of all, it is apparent that these answers are clearly, just from common-sense, incorrect. Secondly, you must be sure to look at the whole sentence to ensure your answer includes all of the required information.

Another example could be a text that translated to the following:

Nowadays, children spend an average of 2 hours and 45 minutes watching TV, and that doesn't even include the half an hour they spend on the internet or playing video games...

And you had to tick one of the boxes below:

Every day, children are in front of a screen for...

- ☐ *Two hours and fifteen minutes*
- ☐ *Two hours and forty-five minutes*
- ☐ *Three hours and fifteen minutes*

...I can guarantee that around 60% of students would tick the second box because they saw this piece of information in the text and jumped to the immediate conclusion that this must be the answer, without paying attention or thinking about the second piece of information given. So, make sure you are part of the 40% of candidates who gets this type of question correct. Avoid falling into the examiners' traps every time and you will be taking a firm step towards boosting your grade.

Note: There are some more ways in which examiners will try to trick you (although these are more common in the listening paper) on pg. 32.

Writing Answers in Spanish

There is, for most exam boards (you should check with your teacher whether your exam board requires you to do this), a question which involves writing answers in Spanish. This section will give you the tools you need to make sure you are able do this.

This is supposed to be one of the most difficult tasks you have to complete in your entire (I)GCSE exam. If you can do this, you immediately put yourself into the top bracket of candidates. To be honest, it really isn't that hard if you know exactly what you have to do. The following system requires minimal knowledge of the Spanish language and will ensure you know the precise techniques needed to gain as many marks as possible.

La salud mental de la gente que vive sola sufre
23 de enero de 2014

Según una investigación llevada a cabo en España, la gente que vive sola es propensa un 70% más a sufrir depresión que aquellos que viven en pareja.

El estudio analizó alrededor de 2,500 casos de depresión y los investigadores han enfatizado el hecho de que el número de familias encabezadas por una sola persona en los países desarrollados ha aumentado en los últimos veintiséis años. Hoy en día, una de cada cuatro personas en los Estados Unidos y el Reino Unido vive sin la compañía de otra.

Durante la investigación se habló con una pensionista, María, que vive cerca de Valencia, quien afirmó: "No me gusta nada vivir sola sin marido ni hijos en casa. Necesito encontrarme a menudo con otros miembros de mi familia o con mis amigas para conservar mi capacidad de conversación." Esta declaración reafirma claramente lo que muestran las estadísticas – sin otra gente en la vida el cerebro sufre.

We have already analysed the above text (here I have only included the first three paragraphs) to deduce its meaning. There were previously no questions to accompany the text. This should have proved to you that you can understand the **vast majority** of any (I)GCSE passage without many tools to help you. However - now that I've convinced you of that - I am going to give you a couple of questions which require answers from the text above, **<u>in Spanish</u>**. (Ignore the highlighting and underlining for now.)

1) ¿Qué ha mostrado el estudio de alrededor de 2500 casos de depresión sobre el número de familias encabezadas por una sola persona en los países avanzados?
[1]

First of all we need to understand the question. In order to do this we use the same methods we used to get the gist of the whole article and look for Spanish words which resemble English ones, and also consider what the question is likely to mean. I have highlighted the words which have obvious English meanings. Now, often questions will contain more information than you really need, so you must deduce which part of the question is really necessary. (I have underlined it for you.) We then need to look, near to the beginning of the text because we are trying to answer the first question and **questions will always be given in the order the answers appear in the passage**, for what the study has shown about the number of families led by one person alone in developed countries. The answer to this is underlined in the first paragraph (on pg. 28).

Tip: We are only looking for one detail shown by the study because the question only has one mark (indicated by [1]) available.

Once you have found all the information you need, the key to answering the question is to use a mixture of:

- Words from the text
- Words from the question
- Your own words

So, using the above highlighting, an answer which would gain the mark available for this question would be:

El estudio ha mostrado que el número de familias encabezadas por una sola persona ha aumentado en los últimos veintiséis años.

Note: Very often students are worried about 'lifting' (i.e. copying directly) from the text and so try to change everything into their own words and in the process lose marks. Examiners do not expect you to rephrase *encabezadas*, so don't try to. Instead, do simple things like using the word *que* to ensure your answer makes grammatical sense. There are no marks on offer for the quality of language used in your answers but the examiner must be able to understand them!

2) ¿Según la pensionista, María, por qué necesita pasar tiempo con miembros de su familia o con sus amigas?
[1]

If we do exactly the same as we did for the first question, we see that this question is asking for the reason why María needs to meet up with members of her family or with her friends. The answer to this is again underlined in the text (on pg. 28), and you should notice that it is found **after** the answer to the first question.

Here we have an issue which we did not come across in the last question and which is incredibly common in (I)GCSE exams. We need to say why *María* needs to meet up with other people, but the article says why *I* need to meet up with other people, because it is María who is speaking. If you 'lift' the answer directly from the text you will get **no marks** because you are giving the reason why *I* need to meet up with others, rather than giving *María*'s reason. I cannot reiterate enough how important the skill of being able to change the information you are given in the text into the person required by the question is. This is so crucial that it is one of my Golden Rules. If you aren't good at this, ask your teacher to practise it with you.

GOLDEN RULE :
KNOW HOW TO MANIPULATE INFORMATION IN THE TEXT
It is crucial your answer makes sense, and if you get this wrong it can be incredibly costly!

So, my answer to this question would be:

Según María necesita encontrarse con miembros de su familia o con sus amigas para conservar su capacidad de conversación.

Easier Reading Examination Questions

We have now addressed every aspect of the harder questions which will appear in your reading exam, but what about the easier ones? These easier questions are effectively a basic vocabulary test. There is a list of the kind of basic vocabulary that examiners are likely to test you on starting on pg. 69. **These lists are by no means extensive vocab lists; you need to learn more than just these!** There is also advice on how to learn vocabulary on pg. 67.

Finally, make sure you obey the following two golden rules. Every year a handful of people drop down a grade or two by not following these rules, regardless of their ability. Please be careful and don't fall into these traps!

Advice contained in the *Listening Examination* section is also applicable here.

GOLDEN RULE :
ANSWER THE QUESTION IN THE RIGHT LANGUAGE AND THE RIGHT TENSE

If the question asks for answers in English, make sure you give them in English. If it asks for them in Spanish, give them in Spanish! Equally, make sure your answer is written in the tense required by the question - this will normally be the tense the question is written in. If you don't do both of these things, you could lose all of the marks available for an entire question.

GOLDEN RULE :
GIVE THE INFORMATION YOU ARE ASKED TO GIVE

If the question asks you to tick 5 boxes, tick 5 boxes. If you have ticked 4 and are not sure of the last one, take a calculated guess. BUT, most importantly, do not tick 6! If you do you will probably lose all of the marks for that question. Equally, you should not write more information than needed or hedge your bets and write two answers. Only the first answer will be marked and, all too often - as I was told by an examiner - students lose marks by writing an incorrect answer before the correct one.
Similarly, if you are asked: *What is Sammy's favourite toy?* make sure you do NOT write down what John's favourite toy is!

Listening Examination

> All of the advice (particularly the Golden Rules) given in the previous *Reading Examination* and *Writing Answers in Spanish* sections applies to the listening exam, so read from pg. 23 if you haven't already.

First of all, you must have read and understood all of the questions that will be answered in the passage you are about to listen to **before** the recording begins to play. You are given plenty of time at the start of the exam and in between passages, so make sure you know exactly what the questions are looking for **before** the passage even starts.

> **Tip:** Underline key words in the questions **before** the passage starts to play. This way, you'll know what information you need to listen out for. Be aware that the passage will probably not use exactly the same word as in the question, so listen out for words with the same or a similar meaning.

But, be careful! Often questions will say something like:

1) Apart from hamburgers, what is Jimmy's favourite food?

It is not uncommon for examiners to see the answer *hamburgers* because some candidates are not careful enough or simply don't bother to read the questions before the start of the passage. Therefore, when they see *favourite food*, and hear the word *hamburgers*, they just write that down in the heat of the moment and quickly rush onto the next question. This is foolish and you cannot afford to throw away easy marks like this!

Once the passage begins to play - as obvious as this may sound - ensure you listen! Make sure you aren't too busy writing down an answer to hear the next part of the passage; it may contain the answer to the next question.

Solution: Write down, next to the answer space, either in English or Spanish, a clear note or word, to remind you of the answer. You are given time at the end of each question and at the end of the exam to come back and change or insert any answers. It is better to have clues to the answers of all 5 parts of a question and get 3 correct, than to only hear 2 parts of the question, and so only score a maximum of 2 marks.

Make sure you listen out for words similar to English words and also for key words in the question. However, be wary that you may hear key words from the question, but the examiners are trying to catch you out using **negatives** and different **tenses**. Therefore, do not assume that the first word or phrase that you hear is the one you need for your answer. For example, if the question were:

2) How much pocket money does Juan receive each week?

... and you heard Juan say:

"Cuando era menor mi madre me daba diez euros cada semana. Sin embargo decidió aumentar esa cantidad y por lo tanto ahora me da veinte euros cada semana"

... it would be easy to think that the answer you need is *10 euros*, because that is the first piece of information you are given which relates to the question. In fact, the answer is *20 euros*.

Similarly, if the question were:

3) How does Alejandra get to school?

... and the passage said the following:

"Alejandra no va al colegio en coche porque le gusta ir en tren para charlar con sus amigas."

... many candidates would write that she goes by car, when in fact the answer is: *She goes by train*.

Finally, there is a list of crucial vocab for your listening exam starting on pg. 69 (they are the same lists as for the easy questions in the reading examination). **These lists are by no means extensive vocab lists; you need to learn more than just these.** However, at the start of the listening exam there will be a number of relatively easy sections where this vocab could come up, and if you want to succeed in the exam it is critical you score very well on these easier sections, so make sure you learn the vocab.

Section II

Tools To Boost Your Grade

Phrases

These phrases are organized into different categories for different time periods of your essay (i.e. past, present and future). You should have these pages open while you are writing any essay in Spanish - at least for now. Remember that you need to show off your use of different tenses, so it is crucial that you use plenty of phrases from each time period over the course of your essay.

Although there are quite a few phrases here, when you have practised using them a couple of times, you should begin to familiarize yourself with the phrases you most like to use. Then, I would advise making your own list of your favourite ones, taking at least 3 phrases from each category. Learn these for your exams.

After that, use these phrases either while preparing for assignments (for standard GCSE) or during the examination itself (for IGCSE).

[verb] = followed by any verb
[inf.] = followed by the infinitive form
(e.g. to do = hacer) of any verb
[pa.p.] = followed by a past participle
(e.g. done = hecho)
[pr.p.] = followed by a present participle
(e.g. doing = haciendo)
[cond.] = followed by conditional
(e.g. I would do = haría)
[subj.] = followed by subjunctive

[noun] = followed by any noun
[adj.] = followed by any adjective

Don't worry too much about why these are used in a particular phrase. Just make sure that when you use a phrase, you also use the correct part of speech. Be careful: Spanish constructions don't always use the same parts of speech as English constructions.

Note: See pg. 47 for the *List of Useful...* section. This will give you lists of each of the parts of speech for you to use with these phrases.

Standard Phrases

Present

1) Suelo **[inf.]** – I normally **[verb]**

   Suelo **pasar** dos semanas en España durante las vacaciones de verano. – I normally **spend** two weeks in Spain during the summer holidays.

2) Tengo que / puedo / quiero **[inf.]** – I have (must) / am able (can) / want **[inf.]**

   Tengo que / puedo / quiero **ponerme** una camiseta blanca cuando hace sol. – I have / am able / want **to wear** a white T-shirt when it is sunny.

3) Trato de **[inf.]** – I try **[inf.]**

   Cuando estoy en casa trato de **ayudar** a mi madre a hacer las tareas. – When I am at home, I try **to help** my mum do the chores.

4) Me encanta **[inf.]**... porque... – I love **[inf.]**... because...

   Me encanta **nadar** en el mar porque es muy bueno para la salud y pienso que es divertidísimo. – I love **to swim** in the sea because it is very healthy and I think that it is very fun.

5) Tengo ganas de **[inf.]** – I feel like **[pr.p.]** / I want **[inf.]**

   Quiero viajar mucho porque tengo ganas de **ver** el mundo. – I want to travel a lot because I feel like **seeing** / I want **to see** the world.

6) Me aburro de **[inf.]** – I get bored of **[pr.p]**

   Hay una gama amplia de tiendas en el centro comercial y por eso nunca me aburro de **ir de compras** con mis amigos. – There is a wide range of shops in the shopping centre and so I never get bored of **shopping** with my friends.

7) Al **[inf.]** – On **[pr.p.]**

   Al **terminar** mis exámenes, fui a la discoteca para encontrarme con mis amigos. – On **finishing** my exams, I went to the disco to meet up with my friends.

8) Acabo de **[inf.]** – I have just **[pa.p.]**

   Acabo de **volver** de España adonde fui de vacaciones con mi familia. – I have just **returned** from Spain where I went on holiday with my family.

9) Para **[inf.]** – In order **[inf.]**

10) En este momento estoy **[pr.p.]** – At the momento, I am **[pr.p.]**

   (9 & 10) En este momento estoy **escribiendo** este libro para **ayudar**os a tener éxito. – At the moment, I am **writing** this book in order **to help** you succeed.

Tip: In Spanish, lots of idiomatic phrases (phrases that Spanish people use in their day-to-day lives) use *tener*. In the previous example, we saw the use of *tener éxito*, meaning *to succeed*. Here is a list of the most useful *tener* phrases. Try to include some of them in your own essays:

- tener hambre – to be hungry
- tener sed – to be thirsty
- tener calor – to be hot
- tener frío – to be cold
- (no) tener razón – to (not) be right
- tener ... años – to be ... years old
- tener miedo de... – to be afraid of...
- tener ganas de... – to feel like…
- tener éxito – to succeed
- tener cuidado – to be careful
- tener suerte – to be lucky
- tener lugar – to take place
- tener en cuenta – to take into account

11) Dudo que **[subj.]** – I doubt that **[verb]**

   Dudo que mi hermano **pueda** venir a Mallorca con mi familia este verano porque tiene que trabajar mucho en su nuevo empleo. – I doubt that my brother **can** come to Majorca with my family this summer because he has to work a lot in his new job.

12) **[present verb]** desde hace **[time expression]** – I have been **[pr.p.]** for **[time expression]**

> **Toco** la guitarra desde hace **diez años**. – I have been **playing** the guitar for **ten years**.

Tip: Make sure you use *tocar* to mean *to play* when talking about a musical instrument and *jugar* when talking about a sport.

13) Hace **[time expression]** – **[time expression]** ago

Note: Obviously this one would be followed by the past, even though it is technically a present expression!

> Hace **cuatro semanas** fui al estadio de Twickenham para ver un partido de rugby. – **Four weeks** ago, I went to Twickenham stadium to watch a rugby match.

14) Me llevo bien / fatal con **[noun]** – I get on well / terribly with **[noun]**

> Me llevo bien con mi **profesor** de español porque siempre hago mis deberes a tiempo. – I get on well with my Spanish **teacher** because I always do my homework on time.

Note: In Spanish, the word for *Spanish* does not begin with a capital letter and so is written as *español*, rather than *Español*. This is the same for all languages / nationalities (i.e. *Germans play football* translates to: *Los alemanes juegan al fútbol).*

15) No soporto… – I cannot stand…

> No soporto a la gente que tira basura en la calle. – I cannot stand people who throw their rubbish into the street.

Note: When this phrase is followed by a person or a group of people, you must remember the personal 'a'. So many students will lose marks by forgetting to use this and will simply write: *No soporto la gente...* See pg. 116 for more information on the personal 'a'.

16) Desde mi punto de vista no se puede negar que... – From my point of view, you can't deny that...

Desde mi punto de vista no se puede negar que la comida rápida causa obesidad. – From my point of view, you can't deny that fast food leads to obesity.

Past

Preterite

1) Decidí **[inf.]** – I decided **[inf.]**

Decidí **comprar** unas postales porque quería mandarlas a mi familia. – I decided **to buy** some postcards because I wanted to send them to my family.

2) Se me ocurrió **[inf.]** – I had the idea of **[pr.p.]**

Mientras navegaba por la red se me ocurrió **hacer** un pastel. – While I was surfing the web, I had the idea of **making** a cake.

3) Pasé mucho tiempo **[pr.p.]** – I spent a lot of time **[pr.p.]**

Pasé mucho tiempo **descansando** con un libro. – I spent a lot of time **relaxing** with a book.

Note: *un* libro – a book   *una* libra (esterlina) – a pound (sterling)

4) Conocí a **[noun]** – I met **[noun]**

i) Conocí a un montón de **chicas** guapas. – I met loads of hot **girls**.

ii) Conocí a un montón de **chicos** guapos. – I met loads of hot **guys**.

Note: When you meet someone for the first time, you use the verb *conocer a*. However, if you meet up with a friend, you use *encontrarse con*. So, you could also use the following in your essay: *El fin de semana pasado me encontré con un amigo... – Last weekend I met a friend...*

5) El año pasado / La semana pasada **+ fui +** al cine / al centro comercial / a España **+** con mi familia / con mis amigos. – Last year / Last week **+ I went +** to the cinema / to the shopping centre / to Spain **+** with my family / with my friends.

6) Me quedé sorprendido de lo poco / mucho que... – I was surprised at how much / little...

En España me quedé sorprendido de lo mucho que usé el transporte público. – In Spain, I was surprised at how much I used public transport.

Imperfect

1) Cuando era más joven **[imperfect]** – When I was younger, I used **[inf.]**

Cuando era más joven **jugaba** al fútbol todos los sábados pero ahora tengo que emplear este tiempo haciendo mis deberes. – When I was younger, I used **to play** football every Saturday, but now I have to spend this time doing my homework.

2) Estaba **[pr.p.]**... cuando **[preterite]** – I was **[pr.p.]**... when **[perfect]**

Estaba **buscando** mis llaves cuando **encontré** mi bufanda. – I was **looking for** my keys when I **found** my scarf.

Note: *Buscar* means *to search for*, not just *to search*. Therefore, the verb is never followed by *por* – a mistake often made by students!

3) Hacía buen / mal tiempo – The weather was nice / bad.

4) Hacía sol / calor / frío. – It was sunny / hot / cold.

5) Nada presagiaba la catástrofe que iba a ocurrir. – There was no hint of the catastrophe that was going to take place.

Nada presagiaba la catastrophe que iba a ocurrir. Sin embargo un minuto más tarde me di cuenta de que había olvidado llevar mi pasaporte. – There was no hint of the catastrophe that was going to take place. However, one minute later I realised that I had forgotten to bring my passport.

General Past

1) Después de **[inf.]** – Having **[pa.p.]**

   Después de **llegar** al centro comercial fuimos al restaurante. – Having **arrived** at the shopping centre, we went to a restaurant.

2) Antes de **[inf.]** – Before **[pr.p.]**

   Antes de **irme** de la biblioteca terminé mi libro. – Before **leaving** the library, I finished my book.

Tip: Don't get confused between *ir a* meaning *to go to* and *irse de* meaning *to leave (from)* – they are similar but normally have very different implications in terms of meaning.

3) Acababa de **[inf.]** – I had just **[pa.p.]**

   Acababa de **hacer** mis deberes cuando decidí ir al parque con mis amigos. – I had just **done** my homework when I decided to go to the park with my friends.

4) Si hubiera tenido más tiempo / dinero, me habría gustado... **[inf.]** – If I had had more time / money, I would have liked to have **[pa.p.]**

   Si hubiera tenido más tiempo, me habría gustado **comprar** un regalo para mi hermana. – If I had had more time, I would have liked to have **bought** a present for my sister.

5) Si hubiera **[pa.p.]**... habría **[pa.p.]**... – If I had **[pa.p.]**.., I would have **[pa.p.]**...

   Si hubiera **sabido** que Sam estaba en España habría **ido** allí también. – If I had **known** that Sam was in Spain, I would have **gone** there as well.

6) ¡Ojalá hubiera podido **[inf.]**..! – If only I could have **[pa.p.]**..!

   ¡Ojalá hubiera podido **ir** a la playa! Sin embargo, desafortunadamente hacía demasiado frío y por lo tanto decidimos quedarnos en casa. – If only I could have **gone** to the beach! However, unfortunately it was too cold and so we decided to stay at home.

7) Me di cuenta de que... – I realised that...

Durante el viaje al aeropuerto me di cuenta de que había olvidado llevar mi pasaporte. – During the journey to the airport I realised that I had forgotten to bring my passport.

Future

1) Voy a **[inf.]** – I am going **[inf.]**

Este fin de semana voy a **trabajar** en una cafetería. – This weekend I am going **to work** in a café.

2) Estoy preparando **[inf.]** – I'm planning **[inf.]**

Estoy preparando **ir** a los Estados Unidos con mis amigos durante las vacaciones de Pascua. – I'm planning **to go** to America with my friends during the Easter holidays.

3) Cuando tenga dieciocho años **[future]** – When I'm eighteen, **[future]**

Note: It is important to remember that when using 'when' to signify a future event (e.g. *when I'm 18...*) in Spanish, you have to use '*cuando [subj.]*'. So you can't just say '*cuando teng**o** dieciocho años*', you have to say '*cuando teng**a** dieciocho años*'.

Cuando tenga dieciocho años **asistiré** a la Universidad de Cambridge. – When I'm eighteen, **I will attend** the University of Cambridge.

4) Cuando sea mayor **[future]** – When I'm older, **[future]**

Cuando sea mayor **compraré** un coche caro. – When I'm older, **I will buy** an expensive car.

5) Espero que **[subj.]** – I hope that **[verb]**

Cuando vaya de vacaciones espero que **haga** calor. – When I go on holiday, I hope that **it's** hot.

Note: For more information on why you must say *ir de vacaciones* in Spanish (*vaya de vacaciones* in the above example), turn to pg. 113.

Conditional

1) Me encantaría **[inf.]** – I would love **[inf.]**

   Cuando tenga deicisiete años me encantaría **aprender** a conducir. – When I'm seventeen, I would love **to learn** to drive.

2) Preferiría **[inf.]** – I would prefer **[inf.]**

   Me gusta ser alto pero preferiría **ser** bajo. – I like being tall but I would prefer **to be** small.

3) Si fuera mayor **[cond.]** – If I were older, **[cond.]**

   Si fuera mayor **iría** a Magaluf con todos mis amigos. – If I were older, I **would go** to Magaluf with all my friends.

4) Si tuviera mucho **[noun]**, **[cond.]** – If I had a lot of **[noun]**, **[cond.]**

   Si tuviera mucho **dinero**, **pasaría** mis vacaciones en hoteles lujosos. – If I had a lot of **money**, **I would spend** my holidays in luxurious hotels.

5) Diría que... – I would say that...

   Diría que lo más importante en la vida es la felicidad. – I would say that the most important thing in life is happiness.

Note: In order to say '*the most / least... thing is...*' in Spanish, it is best not to translate literally! Although the translation of '*the thing*' into Spanish gives '*la cosa*', this is replaced by '*lo*'. So, rather than '*la cosa más importante en la vida es...*', it is '*lo más importante en la vida es...*'. Go to pg. 115 for more.

6) Se debería... – You (in general) should...

   Se debería llegar al lugar de trabajo a tiempo. – You should arrive at your place of work on time.

Opinion Phrases

Present Opinions

1) Me interesa **[inf.]** – I'm interested in **[pr.p.]**

   Me interesa **probar** la comida nueva. – I'm interested in **trying** new food.

2) Creo que es muy **[adj.] [inf.]** – I think that it is very **[adj.] [inf.]**

   Creo que es muy **importante mantenerse** en forma puesto que hay demasiada obesidad hoy en día. – I think that it is very **important to stay** fit because there is too much obesity nowadays.

Note: Although *creo que* translates literally to *I believe*, it is actually used far more regularly than *pienso que* by Spaniards. Having said that, it is good to use both in order to prevent your opinions from sounding repetitive.

3) No creo / pienso / opino que **[subj.]** – I don't think that **[verb]**

   No creo / pienso / opino que el gobierno **priorice** el medio ambiente y por lo tanto nunca se terminará el calentamiento global. – I don't think that the government **prioritises** the environment and so global warming will never be stopped.

4) No me gusta nada el hecho de que **[subj.]** – I don't like the fact that **[verb]**

   No me gusta nada el hecho de que mi madre no me **permita** tocar la batería en mi dormitorio. – I don't like the fact that my mum doesn't **allow** me to play the drums in my bedroom.

5) A mi modo de ver es bueno / absurdo / lamentable / imprescindible / necesario que **[subj.]** – In my opinion, it's good / absurd / sad / essential / necessary that **[verb]**

   A mi modo de ver es absurdo que su jefe le **pague** mal. – In my opinion, it's absurd that his boss **pays** him badly.

   A mi modo de ver es imprescindible que los niños **asistan** al colegio. – In my opinion, it's essential that children **attend** school.

6) La experiencia me resulta **[adj.]** – I find the experience **[adj.]**

Me chifla conducir rápido porque la experiencia me resulta **emocionante**. – I love driving quickly because I find the experience **thrilling**.

7) Al fin y al cabo no me cabe duda de que... – At the end of the day, I don't doubt that...

Al fin y al cabo no me cabe duda de que los seres humanos solucionarán la crisis ambiental. – At the end of the day, I don't doubt that human beings will resolve the environmental crisis.

Past Opinions

1) Lo que más me gustó fue **[inf.]**... porque... – What I most liked was **[pr.p.]**... because...

Lo que más me gustó fue **comprar** nueva ropa porque todo era súper barato. – What I most liked was **buying** new clothes because everything was extremely cheap.

2) Siempre he soñado con **[inf.]** – I have always dreamt of **[pr.p.]**

Me gustaría ir a París porque siempre he soñado con **ir** allí con mi novio / novia. – I would like to go to Paris because I've always dreamt of **going** there with my boyfriend / girlfriend.

3) Me resultó **[adj.] [inf.]**... – I found **[pr.p.]**... **[adj.]**

Me resultó **pesado leer** los libros de J.K. Rowling. – I found **reading** J.K. Rowling's books **tedious**.

4) Fue una experiencia que no olvidaré nunca. – It was an experience that I'll never forget.

5) Fue un día de los que merece la pena recordar toda la vida. – It was one of those days that are worth remembering forever.

6) i) ¡Lo pasé bomba! – I had a great time!
   ii) ¡Lo pasamos bomba! – We had a great time!

CROATIANS – One Acronym to Rule them All

This acronym is a brilliant way to remind you of the tools you should employ while writing any essay in order to boost your grade. Each of the letters of *CROATIANS* represents a different element that is guaranteed to impress any examiner. This acronym is particularly useful if you have to write an unprepared essay in your exam because, by the nature of being under exam pressure, you are likely to forget some of the tools at your disposal if you do not have a reliable way of remembering what they are.

Connectives are a great way to link together your ideas and, crucially, to form longer, more complex sentences that illustrate your ability to expand your ideas.

Reasons are, as has been made clear before, crucial if you want to succeed. The words *porque*, *ya que* and *puesto que* must appear throughout your essay.

Opinion Phrases can be found in the previous section, starting on pg. 44. These are a brilliant tool for showing off complex grammar and, more crucially, are necessary if you want to obtain the best possible mark for Communication.

Adjectives – not just the boring ones! Try to employ a range of adjectives in your essay that demonstrate a greater knowledge of vocabulary and that make you stand out from the rest.

Tenses are vital. You must know and be able to use at least the present, imperfect, preterite and future. (See pg. 81-100 for help on tenses.)

Intensifiers should be used as a way of supplementing adjectives and increasing the complexity of the language you use.

Adverbs of Time are an essential tool for illustrating to the examiner which part of the question you are answering.

Negatives increase the level of sophistication of your essay.

Standard Phrases can be found in the previous section, starting on pg. 36. These will enable you to show-off your knowledge of complex grammar in the knowledge that what you are writing is totally error-free!

List of Useful...

This section is designed to go alongside the previous sections, *Phrases* and *CROATIANS – One Acronym to Rule them All*, by providing you with some parts of speech you can use in phrases and many of the tools listed in *CROATIANS*.

The lists below contain the most common verbs in the Spanish language. You must know and be able to recognize **all** of these in the infinitive form as well as in the basic tenses if you want to maximise your chance of success.

Infinitives

comer – to eat
comprar – to buy
conducir – to drive
dar – to give
deber **[inf.]** – to need/have **[inf.]**
encantar – to love
escuchar – to listen
gustar – to like
hablar – to speak
hacer – to do/make
ir – to go
jugar – to play
leer – to read
nadar – to swim
pensar – to think
poder **[inf.]** – to be able **[inf.]**
poner – to put
preferir – to prefer
quedarse – to stay
querer **[inf.]** – to want **[inf.]**
salir – to leave/go out
tener – to have
terminar – to finish
tomar – to take
trabajar – to work
ver – to see
vivir – to live

Past Participles

comido – eaten
comprado – bought
conducido – driven
dado – given
debido **[inf.]** – needed/had **[inf.]**
encantado – loved
escuchado – listened
gustado – liked
hablado – spoken
hecho – done/made
ido – gone
jugado – played
leído – read
nadado – swum
pensado – thought
podido **[inf.]** – been able **[inf.]**
puesto – put
preferido – preferred
quedado – stayed
querido **[inf.]** – wanted **[inf.]**
salido – left/gone out
tenido – had
terminado – finished
tomado – taken
trabajado – worked
visto – seen
vivido – lived

Present Participles

conduciendo – driving
durmiendo – sleeping
haciendo – doing/making
jugando – playing
teniendo – having
trabajando – working

Conditionals

All in 1st person singular (*I*) form

iría – I would go
habría – I would have
me gustaría – I would like
preferiría – I would prefer

Subjunctives

All in 1st person singular (*I*) form

haga – I do
pueda **[inf.]** – I am able **[inf.]**
quiera **[inf.]** – I want **[inf.]**
tenga – I have
vaya – I go
vea – I see

Connectives & Reason Words

The following table is full of incredibly useful connecting words to help you create the long sentences required in order to achieve the highest **Use of language** mark. They will also allow you to link from one sentence to the next.

Connectives & Reason Words	Meaning	Example
porque / ya que / puesto que (*porque* most common by far)	because	Me encantaría aprender a cocinar **porque / ya que / puesto que** soy admirador de Ferran Adrià.
pero	but	Quiero que venga mi hermana a la fiesta **pero** está ocupada.
por eso / por lo tanto	therefore / so	Su padre es profesor y **por eso / por lo tanto** trabaja muy duro.
luego / después	then / next	Pasamos dos horas en la playa. **Luego / Después** decidimos ir al cine.
cuando	when	**Cuando** hace sol, siempre me pongo una camiseta.
además / también / asimismo / lo que es más / por añadidura	furthermore / moreover / also	Me gustaría casarme con una chica muy talentosa y guapa. **Además / También/ Asimismo / Lo que es más / Por añadidura** tiene que ser tranquila.

sin embargo	however	Es crucial que traigas la crema solar para que no te hagas quemaduras. **Sin embargo**, más importante que nada es tu pasaporte.
dado que / ya que / pues	since / seeing that	Me quedo en casa **dado que / ya que / pues** tengo que estudiar mucho.
a pesar de eso / dicho eso	despite that / having said that	Odio ir de compras. **A pesar de eso / Dicho eso**, fui con mi novia la semana pasada porque a ella le gusta mucho.
en primer lugar	first (of all) / firstly	**En primer lugar**, nos levantamos a las cinco de la mañana.
mientras	while	Hacía sus deberes **mientras** miraba la televisión y por lo tanto su trabajo era mediocre.
mientras que	whereas	Mi padre quiere ir de vacaciones la semana próxima, **mientras que** mi madre preferiría quedarse en casa.
en cuanto a	as for	Yo he hecho el mío pero, **en cuanto a** Juan, tendrá que hacerlo por sí mismo.

Note: Sorry to keep banging on about this, but it is so important that *porque*, *ya que* and *puesto que* are used regularly throughout your essays so that you ensure you are giving:

- Justifications for why you did things
- What you thought of the things you did
- Why you have that opinion

Adjectives

Remember that all these adjectives (and any you look up) are given in the masculine singular form. If you use them in an essay, ensure you make them agree with the noun they are describing - including yourself if you're a girl - in both gender (masculine / feminine) and number (singular / plural). Asterisks (*) denote that an adjective is invariable for masculine and feminine forms.

Feelings, Emotions & Opinions

amable* / simpático – kind
bonito – beautiful
cansado – tired
contento – happy / satisfied
desanimado – disheartened
divertido – fun

encantado – delighted
enfermo – ill
relajante* – relaxing
sano – healthy
triste* – sad

Note: These will often follow the verb *to be* (e.g. *I was sad*). In English, there is only one way of saying *to be*, but in Spanish there are two: *ser* and *estar*. The difficulty is in knowing which one of these verbs to use. There is a very comprehensive explanation of when to use *ser* and *estar* starting on pg. 108.

Overused Opinions

Some adjectives used to express opinion are overused and unimpressive to examiners. Sometimes, a particular word (even if it's a bit unimpressive) has to be used in order to get across the intended meaning. However, if another makes sense, replace the more boring word with one of these:

interesante* – interesting
cautivador – captivating
educativo – educational
encantador – charming
impresionante* – impressive

malo – bad
abominable* – appalling
espantoso – atrocious
fatal* – terrible
malísimo – rubbish

bueno – good
estupendo – wonderful
fabuloso – fabulous
fenomenal* – awesome
genial* – terrific
incredible* – astonishing
sensacional* – sensational

aburrido – boring
fastidioso – annoying / tiresome
pesado – dull / tedious

Intensifiers

muy – very
demasiado – too
mucho – a lot / much
bastante – quite
un poco – a bit

más – more
menos – less
verdaderamente – really
particularmente – particularly
sorprendentemente – remarkably

Adverbs of Time

siempre – always
todos los días – every day
a menudo – often
generalmente – usually
a veces – sometimes

de vez en cuando – from time to time / every now and then
rara vez – rarely
nunca – never
luego / después – then / next

More Adverbs of Time

At the moment		In the past	
anteayer	the day before yesterday	**dos días antes**	two days before
ayer	yesterday	**el día anterior**	the day before
hoy	today	**aquel día**	(on) that day
mañana	tomorrow	**al día siguiente**	(on) the next day
pasado mañana	the day after tomorrow	**dos días después**	two days later

Time Expressions

Here is a list of 11 basic time expressions. You should always use these in essays and oral conversations to show the examiner whether you are talking about the past, present or future.

Past
- hace tres meses...
  – three months ago...
- la semana pasada...
  – last week...
- el fin de semana pasado...
  – last weekend...
- el verano pasado...
  – last summer...
- durante... – during...

Present
- hoy en día... – nowadays...
- actualmente... – currently...
- ahora... – now...

Future
- el año que viene...
  – next year...
- cuando tenga dieciocho años... – when I'm 18...
- este fin de semana...
  – this weekend...

Negatives

- no – not
  No quiero jugar al baloncesto. – I do **not** want to play basketball.
- ya no – no longer
  Mi hermana menor **ya no** tiene que beber leche cada mañana. – My younger sister **no longer** has to drink milk every morning.
- no... nada – nothing
  No hay **nada** malo en levantarse temprano. – There is **nothing** wrong with getting up early.
- nunca / no... nunca – never
  Sin embargo, **nunca** me levanto temprano. / Sin embargo, **no** me levanto **nunca** temprano. – However, I **never** get up early.
- nadie – nobody
  Nadie sabe lo que yo debería hacer. – **Nobody** knows what I should do.
- ni... ni – neither... nor
  Ni tengo trabajo **ni** dinero. – I have **neither** work **nor** money.

Combining Negatives

Mi hermano **nunca** dice **nada** a **nadie**. – My brother **never** says **anything** to **anyone**.

Sentence Structure Formula

You hopefully remember that in order to boost your mark for **Use of language** you need to use longer sentences. This is true... **BUT** do not make them more than a few lines long or you will begin to make mistakes and they will become confusing.

So, what you need to do is: try to use a combination of phrases (often a standard phrase with an opinion phrase) in order to produce more complex sentences. You can then link these phrases and sentences together with time expressions and connecting words.

Here is an example of how this works:

Present phrase	Suelo pasar tres semanas en España con mi familia
porque, puesto que or *ya que*	porque
Opinion phrase	me encanta jugar con mi hermano en la playa
Connecting word	sin embargo,
Time expression	este año
Past phrase	decidí ir de vacaciones con mis amigos
porque, puesto que or *ya que*	ya que
Opinion phrase	siempre he soñado con viajar sin mis padres.

Clearly, the above is not a hard-and-fast structure which you have to use for every single sentence you write; evidently that would be ridiculous. However, it ought to give you an example of how you can string together plenty of the different structures I have shown you. I can tell you with absolute certainty that doing so correctly will greatly boost your mark in any (I)GCSE essay or oral examination. Using this idea, you ought to get into the habit of giving reasons for virtually everything you say by using a mixture of standard phrases, opinion phrases and the words *porque*, *puesto que* or *ya que*.

Sample Essay Question

Here is a sample essay on holidays, packed full of great expressions. You will find a key to the colour coding at the bottom of the next page. The task / title is as follows:

You recently travelled to Spain on holiday. Write about your visit, including:

- *What you normally do for your holidays*
- *How you travelled to Spain*
- *What you saw and did as well as your opinion of Spanish food*
- *Where you will go on future holidays and why*

[1]**Durante las vacaciones** [6]**suelo** pasar dos semanas con mis amigos en Francia [5]**porque** los vuelos son baratos y [4]**creo que** las playas son muy bonitas. [7]**Aunque** [6]**tengo que** gastar mucho dinero, [4]**prefiero** ir de vacaciones con mis amigos [5]**porque** puedo salir a las discotecas con ellos [7]**y por eso** [4]**es muy divertido**.

[2]**El verano pasado** fui a España con mi familia y pasamos unas vacaciones [6]**llenas de actividades**. Fuimos en coche, lo que [4]**me resultó** bastante aburrido pero [4]**me encantó** ver el paisaje magnífico de España.

Fuimos a la playa cuando hacía sol y [4]**lo que más me gustó fue** nadar en el mar [5]**ya que** el agua estaba fría y [6]**estuvimos a treinta grados**. [4]**Me encanta** nadar [5]**porque** es muy bueno para la salud y [4]**pienso que** es divertidísimo. [7]**También** [4]**me gustó** tomar el sol [5]**porque** [6]**siempre he soñado con** tener la piel morena. [7]**Además** [6]**pasé mucho tiempo** descansando con un libro, [7]**así que** leí tres libros de Harry Potter.

[1]**During the holidays** [6]**I normally** spend two weeks with my friends in France [5]**because** the flights are cheap and [4]**I think that** the beaches are very beautiful. [7]**Although** [6]**I have to** spend lots of money, [4]**I prefer** going on holiday with my friends [5]**because** I can go out to nightclubs with them [7]**and so** [4]**it is great fun**.

[2]**Last summer**, I went to Spain with my family and we had a holiday [6]**full of activities**. We went by car, which [4]**I found** quite boring but [4]**I loved** looking at Spain's magnificent scenery.

We went to the beach when it was sunny and [4]**what I most liked was** swimming in the sea [5]**because** the water was cold and [6]**it was thirty degrees**. [4]**I love** swimming [5]**because** it's very good for my health and [4]**I think that** it's very fun. [7]**Also**, [4]**I liked** sunbathing [5]**because** [6]**I've always dreamt of** having tanned skin. [7]**Furthermore**, [6]**I spent a lot of time** relaxing with a book, [7]**and so** I read three Harry Potter books.

[2]El sábado conocí a una chica guapa/ un chico guapo que me dio la comida típica del país. [4]Para mí, [6]fue una experiencia que no olvidaré nunca. Tomamos paella. [4]¡Qué rica!

[2]On Saturday, I met a good-looking girl/ a good-looking boy who gave me some typical food from the country. [4]For me, [6]it was an experience that I will never forget. We had paella. [4]How delicious!

[3]El año que viene [6]estoy preparando ir a España con mis amigos. [5]Estoy seguro de que [4]lo pasaremos bomba si hace buen tiempo, [7]aunque la verdad es que [8]si tuviera más dinero, preferiría quedarme en un hotel lujoso en el centro de París. [8]Cuando tenga dieciocho años, iré a los Estados Unidos [5]puesto que, [4]en mi opinión, la experiencia [4]me resultaría enriquecedora. [7]Asimismo [4]me gustaría quedarme allí [5]ya que [4]me interesa mucho probar la comida típica americana.

[3]Next year, [6]I'm planning on going to Spain with my friends. [5]I'm sure that [4]we'll have a great time if the weather is nice, [7]although the truth is that [8]if I had more money, I would prefer to stay in a luxurious hotel in the centre of Paris. [8]When I'm eighteen, I'll go to the U.S.A. [5]because, [4]in my opinion, [4]I would find the experience enriching. [7]Moreover, [4]I would like to stay there [5]because [4]I'm very interested in trying typical American food.

[1]- Adverb of time shows you are answering the 1st bullet point in the present.
[2]- Adverbs of time show you are answering the 2nd & 3rd bullet points in the past.
[3]- Adverb of time shows you are answering the 4th bullet point in the future and conditional.
[4]- Opinion phrase
[5]- Reason in order to explain why you have an opinion about something
[6]- Very natural 'standard' Spanish phrase
[7]- Connecting word
[8]- Subjunctive... **MARKS!!**

Notice that throughout this sample essay, the spread of different colours is fairly even with:

- A mixture of standard phrases, opinion phrases and reasons for these opinions
- Plenty of connecting words and time expressions
- A few subjunctives to really boost the **Use of language** mark

When you write essays, the key is to manipulate phrases to suit the essay title, just as I have done in this sample essay. Looking at the sample essay again, with the mark scheme (which gives marks for: **Communication, Use of language** and **Accuracy**) in mind, we can see that:

1. There are 5 paragraphs in response to the 4 bullet points (I split one bullet point into two parts). Tenses are used correctly throughout each paragraph. Each paragraph responds specifically to each part of the essay title. The essay is easy to understand and makes sense. Therefore, it will be awarded **full marks** for **Communication**.

2. There are plenty of constructions, all correctly used, which add fluidity to the essay. A few subjunctives are also thrown in! So, **full marks** for **Use of language**.

3. There are no spelling mistakes and there are no mistakes in the use of tenses. All verbs agree with their subjects (the thing doing the verb) and all adjectives agree with their nouns. (This was made easier by using the checking rule on the next page.) Therefore, it would be given **full marks** for **Accuracy**. Please be aware that, although there are no mistakes in this essay, you will be allowed to make some relatively small mistakes and still be awarded full - or close to full - marks for **Accuracy** in your exam. You are not expected to be perfect!

… Finally, I would like to emphasise the point I made right at the start of this guide: You do **not** (in reality) have to have done everything you write about in your essay. You will probably have noticed, in my sample essay, that I wrote about going on holiday with my friends and liking this because I can go clubbing with them. I can say for a fact that I have never been on holiday with friends and gone out clubbing because, aside from the fact I am nowhere near that cool, it's also illegal! The reason I included that sentence was to make you realise and remember that your essay absolutely does not have to be factually correct... You **must** make it up to show off your use of Spanish!

The Checking Rules

··

You now know how to boost your mark for **Communication** and **Use of language**, but how can you improve your **Accuracy** mark?

I am afraid, unless you want to spend hours learning vocabulary lists, I cannot help you with your spelling. However, there is an essay checking formula which, once you have written an essay, should be used without exception. It is in **2 parts**:

PART 1:

- Have your completed essay in front of you and take out a pencil.
- Underline each verb (word of doing) (e.g. *habla* – *he speaks*)... Make sure you don't miss one out!
- Now, go back to the top of the essay, to the first underlined verb.
- Ask yourself four questions about this verb:
  - What is the verb supposed to say in English? (e.g. *he speaks*)
  - What tense is the verb in, in English? (e.g. *he speaks* is present)
  - What person (I, you (sg.), he / she / it, we, you (pl.), they) is that verb, in English? (e.g. *he*)
  - What is the infinitive (i.e. the '*to*' form of the verb) in English, then in Spanish? (e.g. *to speak* – *hablar*)
- Now you need to check the ending of the verb using your knowledge of verb conjugation. Make sure you are comparing it with the correct tense of the correct type of verb (-*ar*, -*er* or -*ir*).

Tip: If there are two verbs next to each other (e.g. *he ido*) and the first is part of *haber* (e.g. *he*), the second must be a past participle (e.g. *ido*). Otherwise, the second verb must be an infinitive (e.g. *quiero salir*).

- Rub out the pencil under this verb and correct it if you were wrong.
- Repeat the process on every verb.

Note: For more explanation on the use of different tenses and how to construct them, have a look at the *Verbs* section which starts on pg. 80.

PART 2:

- Having completed Part 1, go back to the start of your essay (don't worry, this won't take as long as Part 1) and underline, in pencil, every adjective (descriptive word) (e.g. *bonita – pretty*) and carry out the following procedure on every word now underlined:
- Make sure that the adjective you are using is correctly positioned with respect to the noun it describes. (Should that adjective go before or after the noun?) There is an explanation of adjectival positioning on pg. 102.
- Ask yourself: "What noun is this adjective describing?" (e.g. *una chica* or *un chico*)
  - Is that noun masculine or feminine? (If you don't know whether a noun is masculine or feminine, just make an informed guess. Have a look at *The Rules of Sex* section on pg. 106 for help on this.)

Tip: Remember that there are some nouns that look masculine when they are in fact feminine and vice versa (e.g. *la mano, el problema*). See pg. 106 for a full list of these.

  - Is the noun singular or plural? (Is there one or more than one?)
- Using your answers to the questions above, apply the following rule which works for the **vast majority** of Spanish adjectives:
  - If the masculine singular form of the adjective - the one given in the dictionary - ends in an '*o*' (*bonito*):
    - Feminine singular noun described: replace '*o*' with '*a*' (*bonita)*
    - Masculine plural noun described: add '*s*' (*bonitos*)
    - Feminine plural noun described: replace '*o*' with '*as*' (*bonitas*)
  - If the adjective given in the dictionary ends in an '*e*' (*importante*):
    - Singular masculine or feminine noun: remains the same
    - Plural masculine or feminine noun: add '*s*' (*chicos importantes*)
  - If the adjective given in the dictionary ends in a consonant (*popular*):
    - Singular masculine or feminine noun: remains the same
    - Plural masculine or feminine noun: add '*es*' (*chicas populares*)
- Correct any mistakes you may have made in the agreement of that adjective and rub out the pencil mark under that word.
- Repeat the process on every adjective.

Points to Remember for the Writing Exam

- **Be creative!** You can make up anything you want, as long as you know how to say it and it is relevant to the essay title.

- **Don't miss anything out!** Write a paragraph per bullet point or per part of the essay title (depending on the form in which the task / title is given to you).

- **Remember *CROATIANS*!**
  - **C**onnectives to form longer sentences.
  - **R**easons to justify why you have / had a certain opinion.
  - **O**pinion Phrases to express your thoughts.
  - **A**djectives – not just the boring ones!
  - **T**enses to answer each part of the question.
  - **I**ntensifiers to supplement adjectives.
  - **A**dverbs of Time to show which part of the question you are answering.
  - **N**egatives to increase the sophistication of your essay.
  - **S**tandard Phrases to show off your knowledge of complex grammar.

- **Sound Spanish!** Use both standard phrases and opinion phrases but make sure you don't force them.

- **Always justify!** Every time you give an opinion it must be justified with a reason.

- **Check your work!** Use the Checking Rules to make sure your work is as error-free as it can possibly be. Ensure you leave yourself enough time to do this and try imagining you are finding faults in your arch-nemesis's work!

> YOU MAY NOT HAVE TO DO THIS. If your teacher has not told you about preparing a picture for your oral presentation, skip this page!

Oral Picture Presentation

Firstly, it is important that you choose a picture or photograph that is going to show off your knowledge and that makes the examiner's life easy by containing lots to talk about. I would recommend an image with plenty of action and people included in it. During your preparation, you should prepare a sentence or two to describe what each person or object is doing in the picture as well as a sentence about each person in general (e.g. their personality, hobbies etc.). This covers some of the starter questions the examiner is likely to ask you.

If you have to describe an image in your oral examination (as your presentation), here are some phrases for describing a picture:

- Mi madre sacó esta foto cuando... – My mum took this photo when...
- El año pasado... – Last year...
- Durante un viaje de estudios – During a school trip
- Como se puede ver en la imagen... – As you can see in the photo...
- Esta foto muestra... – This photo shows...
- Esta escena tuvo lugar... – This scene took place...
- Con varios miembros de mi familia – With several members of my family
- Cuando alquilamos un piso en España – When we rented an apartment in Spain
- A la izquierda vemos a mi hermano que... – On the left, we see my brother who...

Here are some position words to describe a photo:

- a la izquierda – on the left
- a la derecha – on the right
- al lado de – next to
- cerca de – near to
- en primer plano – in the foreground
- al fondo – in the background

Tip: Make sure you get the gender of *la foto* and *la imagen* correct.

Oral Exam Questions by Topic Area

Here is a list of virtually every question you could be asked in your (I)GCSE examination. The questions are split up into different oral topic areas. If you are doing a standard GCSE, you should only prepare questions which are related to your task(s). However, for IGCSE, you may be asked any of these questions and so should prepare answers for most of them (**if they are on your syllabus**).

Topic Area I – Home & Abroad

Describe la región donde vives.
¿Te gusta tu región? ¿Por qué?
¿Qué cosas pueden hacer los jóvenes donde vives?
¿Qué has hecho en tu región recientemente?
¿Qué se puede hacer en tu región en verano / invierno?
Si yo fuera un turista, ¿qué me aconsejarías visitar / hacer / ver en tu región?
¿Preferirías vivir en una ciudad o en el campo? ¿Por qué?

¿Qué tiempo hace hoy?
¿Qué tiempo hace generalmente aquí?
¿Qué cosas sueles hacer cuando hace calor / frío?

¿Qué medios de transporte hay en tu región?
¿Qué piensas del transporte público en tu región?
¿Muchas personas usan a menudo el transporte público donde vives?
¿Crees que se podría mejorar los medios de transporte? ¿Cómo?

¿Qué haces normalmente durante las vacaciones? ¿Vas al extranjero?
¿Prefieres ir de vacaciones con tus padres o con tus amigos?
¿Adónde fuiste de vacaciones el año pasado?
¿Cómo viajaste? ¿Dónde te quedaste? ¿Qué hiciste? ¿Qué tiempo hizo?
¿Has visitado algún país hispanohablante? ¿Hablaste mucho español?
¿Adónde vas a ir de vacaciones este año?
¿Qué vas a hacer en tus próximas vacaciones?
Describe las vacaciones de tus sueños.
¿Qué piensas del camping? ¿Lo has hecho antes?

¿Cuáles son las principales fiestas de tu país?
¿Te gusta mucho la Navidad?
¿Qué hiciste el año pasado para celebrar tu cumpleaños?
En tu opinión, ¿son importantes las fiestas? ¿Por qué?

Topic Area II – School & Work Life

Describe tu colegio.
¿Te gusta tu instituto?
¿Qué haces normalmente durante el recreo?
¿Cuáles son tus asignaturas preferidas?
¿Quieres estudiar una asignatura que no ofrece tu instituto?

¿Qué haces en un día típico en el instituto?
Describe uno de tus profesores.
¿Qué significa ser buen profesor para ti?
¿Crees que el uniforme escolar debería ser obligatorio? ¿Por qué?

¿Recibes muchos deberes en tu instituto?
¿Cuándo haces tus deberes?
¿Qué deberes hiciste ayer?
¿Son importantes los deberes? ¿Por qué (no)?
Si pudieras ser director de tu instituto por un día, ¿qué cambiarías? ¿Por qué?

¿Qué vas a hacer después de tus exámenes este año?
¿Qué vas a hacer después del instituto? ¿Quieres estudiar más?
¿Vas a ir a la universidad cuando termines tus estudios escolares? ¿Qué te gustaría estudiar allí?

¿Has tenido un empleo?
¿Trabajas los fines de semana o durante las vacaciones? ¿Qué haces?
¿Qué piensas de tu trabajo? ¿Cuánto ganas?
¿En qué gastas tu dinero?
Para ti, ¿es mejor gastar o ahorrar dinero?

¿Hay un empleo que te gustaría hacer en el futuro? ¿Por qué?
¿Te gustaría trabajar en el extranjero?
¿Cómo sería tu trabajo ideal? ¿Por qué?
¿Crees que el dinero lleva a la felicidad?
En tu opinión, ¿qué es lo más importante de un trabajo?
¿Hay mucho paro en tu región? ¿Es un problema entre los jóvenes que conoces?

Topic Area III – House, Home & Daily Routine

¿Vives en una casa o en un piso?
Describe tu casa / tu piso.
¿Cómo es tu dormitorio?
Si tuvieras mucho dinero, ¿cómo sería tu casa ideal?

¿Cuántas personas hay en tu familia?
Describe a tu padre / tu madre / tu hermano / tu hermana.
Dime algo sobre la personalidad de un miembro de tu familia.
¿Cómo sería tu familia ideal?
¿Te llevas bien con toda la familia?

¿Quién es tu mejor amigo / amiga? Descríbele/la.
¿Conoces a esta persona desde hace mucho tiempo?
¿Cuáles son las virtudes y los desperfectos de tu mejor amigo / amiga?
¿Qué has hecho con tu mejor amigo / amiga recientemente?
¿Vas a hacer algo con tus amigos el fin de semana que viene?
¿Te gustaría ir de vacaciones con tus amigos?

¿A qué hora te levantas por la mañana?
¿Qué hiciste esta mañana antes de ir al instituto?
¿Qué vas a hacer esta tarde cuando vuelvas a casa?
¿Qué suele hacer tu familia el fin de semana?
¿Te gustaría cambiar tu rutina diaria?

¿Qué haces para ayudar en casa?
¿Qué hiciste recientemente para ayudar en casa?
En casa, ¿quién se ocupa la mayoría de las tareas domésticas?

¿Qué has desayunado esta mañana?
¿Tienes una comida / bebida preferida?
¿Hay algo que no te guste comer / beber?
¿Comes en el comedor del instituto? ¿Sirven buena comida allí?
¿Qué comiste ayer por la tarde?
¿Quién cocina en casa? ¿Ayudas a preparar la comida?
¿Piensas que los jóvenes deberían aprender a cocinar?
¿Has comido en un restaurante recientemente? ¿Qué tomaste?
¿Qué tipo de cocina te gusta? ¿Por qué?
¿Piensas que comes saludablemente?
¿Por qué hay tanta obesidad hoy en día?
Si fueras ministro de salud, ¿qué harías para reducir la obesidad?

Topic Area IV – The Modern World

¿Has reciclado alguna vez? Explícame lo que has hecho.
¿Por qué es tan importante reciclar hoy en día?
¿Qué has hecho recientemente para proteger el medio ambiente?
En tu instituto / tu región, ¿qué se hace para proteger el medio ambiente?
¿Hay cosas que no haces ahora que podrías hacer? ¿Cuáles son?
¿Qué causa la contaminación atmosférica en general?
¿Crees que tenemos que hacer más para proteger nuestro planeta?
En tu opinión, ¿cuál es el problema más importante con respecto al medio ambiente? ¿Por qué?
¿Qué problemas va a causar en tu país el calentamiento global?

¿Te gusta ver la tele? ¿Pasas mucho tiempo delante de una pantalla?
¿Cuáles son tus tipos de programas favoritos? ¿Por qué?
¿Viste la tele anoche? ¿Qué viste?
¿Qué vas a ver después de volver a casa hoy?
¿Qué prefieres, la radio o la televisión? ¿Por qué?
¿Crees que los jóvenes de hoy en día ven demasiado la tele?
¿Ves las noticias a menudo?
¿Ha pasado recientemente algo importante en tu país que has descubierto por la tele?
¿Lees los periódicos a menudo? ¿Por qué (no)?
¿Cómo se llama el periódico que lees? ¿Qué piensas de él?
¿Qué opinas de la publicidad en la tele? ¿Te molesta?

¿Qué género de películas prefieres? ¿Por qué?
¿Vas al cine a menudo?
Describe la última vez que fuiste al cine. ¿Qué viste? ¿Cómo fue?
¿Dónde prefieres ver una película, en el cine o en la tele? ¿Por qué?

¿Tienes móvil?
¿Cuáles son las ventajas y las desventajas de los móviles?
¿Crees que se debería prohibir el uso de móviles en el colegio?
Si no tuvieras un móvil, ¿Piensas que tu vida sería más difícil?
En el futuro, ¿cómo van a cambiar los móviles?

¿Has utilizado un ordenador recientemente? ¿Para qué?
¿Cuáles son las ventajas y los inconvenientes de los ordenadores?
¿Utilizas Internet? ¿Cuándo? ¿Para qué?
¿Cuáles son las ventajas y las desventajas de Internet?
¿Crees que los ordenadores dominan las vidas de los jóvenes hoy en día?
¿Qué papel van a tener los ordenadores en el futuro?

Topic Area V – Social Activities, Fitness & Health

¿Cuándo es tu cumpleaños?
¿Cómo has celebrado tu cumpleaños en los últimos años?
¿Tienes algunos planes para celebrar el final de tus exámenes este año?

¿Qué te gusta hacer en tu tiempo libre? ¿Por qué te gusta hacerlo?
Tienes una actividad de ocio favorita.
Cuando eras más joven, ¿cuáles eran tus pasatiempos favoritos?
¿Qué deportes practicas? ¿Te gustan?
¿Eres miembro de un club?
¿Hay bastante que hacer para los jóvenes en tu región?
¿Hay algo que no se puede hacer ahora en tu región que te gustaría que introdujera el ayuntamiento?

¿Qué hiciste ayer por la tarde después del colegio?
¿Qué vas a hacer esta tarde?
¿Sales a menudo con tus amigos? ¿Adónde vas? ¿Cuándo?
¿Saliste el fin de semana pasado? ¿Con quién? ¿Qué hiciste?
Describe el fin de semana de tus sueños.

¿Qué prefieres leer: libros, periódicos o revistas?
¿Qué genero de libro prefieres?
¿Qué has leído recientemente? ¿Te gustó?
¿Tocas algún instrumento musical?
¿Qué tipo de música prefieres?
¿Cuál es tu grupo o tu cantante preferido? ¿Por qué?
¿Escuchas música a menudo?
¿Hay una persona famosa que admires?

¿Te gusta mucho hacer shopping?
¿Cuál es tu tienda favorita? ¿Por qué? ¿Qué se puede comprar allí?
¿Te dan tus padres mucho dinero? ¿Cuánto cada semana?
¿Qué has comprado últimamente con tu dinero?

En tu opinión, ¿es importante mantenerte en forma o no?
¿Qué sueles hacer para mantenerte en forma?
¿Qué hacen tus amigos / tus padres para mantenerse en forma?
¿Tienes amigos que no están en buena forma física?
Si te pones enfermo, ¿qué tienes que hacer? ¿Irías al médico?
¿Conoces a personas que fuman? ¿Qué piensas del tabaco?
¿Por qué empieza a tomar drogas mucha gente? ¿Deberían ser castigados?
¿Por qué crees que la gente se hace vegetariana?

Section III

Specific Essential Learning

Vocabulary

There are a few condensed vocab lists starting on pg. 69. These contain words which are likely to come up in the reading and listening papers, particularly in the first few sections. You must learn these lists thoroughly as all of this vocab is certainly expected of you at (I)GCSE. (However, this is not a guarantee that it will definitely come up!) It is also important that you realise that these lists are nowhere near exhaustive and that you must do your own vocab learning if you want to succeed in your Spanish exams.

There is some essential vocab which you simply cannot do without (obviously you aren't going to understand anything without some core knowledge of the basics.) There are tonnes of fairly extensive vocab lists online or in GCSE vocab books. Regardless of which vocab lists you choose to use, I would advise you to go through the most important sections (such as topics you are likely to want to write an essay on or speak about in your oral), highlighting vocab you don't know. Then, follow my three Golden Rules for learning vocabulary:

GOLDEN RULE :
LEARN IT IN SMALL CHUNKS, BUT REGULARLY

I would advise learning 4-7 words only, but learning them daily. Have a list of words which you want to learn on a sheet (print off a GCSE vocab list from your exam board for example) and highlight all the ones you are not 100% certain of on one day. (This might take a bit of time - why not go and do it now?) Then, each day for around 10 minutes - perhaps while eating breakfast or before going to bed - learn 4-7 of those words (you decide exactly how many). Test yourself, and once you can remember the English translation of each Spanish word, you're done for the day.

GOLDEN RULE :
COME UP WITH WAYS OF REMEMBERING WORDS

It's hard to just learn stuff which has no significance to you, for example a random list of words. Therefore, I use little sayings, which are really weird (**BUT** they work for me) to help me remember vocab. For example, *aterrizar* means *to land*; I remember this: 'When the plane lands, find me at Terry's bar', because *aterrizar* sounds like *at Terry's bar*!

GOLDEN RULE :
REVISE VOCAB

Learning vocab can be incredibly dull, but it is vital. It is easy to become frustrated when you have learnt 5 words one day and then, within 3 days, have forgotten them completely. So, in the first Golden Rule, I said to learn 4-7 words a day, but this would mean you forgot the vast majority of the vocab within a week. Therefore, every 4 or 5 days, don't learn anything new. Instead, spend 10 minutes testing yourself on the vocab you have been learning over the past few days. Then, any words which you have forgotten (there will probably be a few) should be underlined and re-learnt as if they were new to you (as one of your 4-7 daily words).

All this might sound complicated, but it really isn't. Just spend a few minutes every day doing it and it will automatically become part of your routine. Just think how much you will learn from such a small amount of time every day: within a year you will have learnt at least 600 words.

Basic Vocab

Los deportes y los pasatiempos – Sports and Hobbies

ajedrez (m)	chess
atletismo (m)	athletics
bailar	to dance
baile (m)	dancing
baloncesto (m)	basketball
caballo (m)	horse
montar a caballo , ir a caballo	to ride (horse)
equitación (f)	horse riding
ciclismo (m)	cycling
escalada (f)	climbing
esquí (m)	skiing
esquí acuático (m)	water skiing
fútbol (m)	football
hacer la vela , practicar la vela	to sail
velero (m) , barco de vela (m)	sailing boat
jugar	to play
nadar	to swim
natación (f)	swimming
patinaje sobre hielo (m)	ice skating
pescar	to fish
practicar	to practise
tenis (m)	tennis
tenis de mesa (m) , ping pong (m)	table tennis
tiro con arco (m)	archery

Note: You cannot say *jugar deportes* to mean *to play sport*. In English it is acceptable to say *play sport*, but in Spanish this is grammatically incorrect. Therefore, you must say *to do sport*, so it's *hacer deportes*.

El aspecto y la personalidad – Appearance and Personality

El aspecto	Appearance
alto	tall
bajo	short (person)
blanco	white
bonito	handsome , pretty
castaño	chestnut
corto	short (hair)
delgado	thin
feo	ugly
fuerte	strong
gordo	fat
guapo	hot , beautiful
largo	long
moreno	dark-skinned , dark-haired
negro	black
obeso	obese
pelirrojo	red-head
pelo (m)	hair
pequeño	small
piel (f)	skin
rubio	blond

La personalidad	Personality
amable , simpático	kind , pleasant
divertido	fun , funny
egoísta	selfish
inteligente	intelligent
orgulloso	proud , arrogant
perezoso	lazy
serio	serious
tímido	shy

El tiempo y las estaciones – Weather and Seasons

El tiempo	Weather
boletín meteorológico (m)	weather report
buen tiempo (m)	good weather
calor (m)	heat
caluroso	hot (climate , season)
cielo (m)	sky
frío	cold
grado (m)	degree (temperature)
llueve , está lloviendo	it is raining
lluvia (f)	rain
lluvioso	rainy
mal tiempo (m)	bad weather
niebla (f)	foggy
nieva , está nevando	it is snowing
nieve (f)	snow
nube (f)	cloud
nublado	cloudy
relámpagos (m pl)	lightning
seco	dry
sol (m)	sun
soleado	sunny
tormenta (f)	storm

Las estaciones	Seasons
invierno (m)	winter
otoño (m)	autumn
primavera (f)	spring
verano (m)	summer

Note: To say *it is* followed by some sort of weather (e.g. *it is sunny*) you say *hace* **NOT** *es* or *está*. Similarly, to say *it was* (e.g. *it was windy*) you must use *hacía* **NOT** *era* or *estaba*. Also, notice that you use the imperfect here, **NOT** the preterite. So, you almost never say: *hizo sol*, but instead say: *hacía sol*.

La ropa y la moda – Clothing and Fashion

La ropa	Clothing
abrigo (m) , chaqueta (f)	coat
bañador (m)	swimming trunks
billetero (m) , cartera (f)	wallet
bolso de mano (m)	handbag
bufanda (f)	scarf
calcetín (m)	sock
camisa (f)	shirt
camiseta (f)	T-shirt
chándal (m)	tracksuit
cinturón (m)	belt
corbata (f)	tie
falda (f)	skirt
gorra (f)	cap
guante (m)	glove
impermeable (m)	raincoat
monedero (m)	purse
pantalón (m)	trousers
paraguas (m)	umbrella
sombrero (m)	hat
suéter (m) , jersey (m)	sweater , jumper
traje (m)	suit
traje de baño (m)	swimming costume

La moda	Fashion
(de) algodón	(made of) cotton
(de) cuero	(made of) leather
(de) lana	(made of) wool
moteado	spotted
rayado , a rayas	stripy
(de) seda	(made of) silk

Las asignaturas – Subjects

alemán (m)	German
arte (m) , dibujo (m)	art
biología (f)	biology
ciencias (f pl)	sciences
diseño (m)	DT
educación física (f)	PE
enseñanza religiosa (f)	religious studies
español (m)	Spanish
física (f)	physics
francés (m)	French
geografía (f)	geography
historia (f)	history
informática (f)	ICT
inglés (m)	English
lenguas extranjeras (f pl)	foreign languages
matemáticas (f pl)	maths
química (f)	chemistry
teatro (m)	drama

El transporte – Transport

a pie	on foot
(en) avión (m)	(by) plane
(en) barco (m)	(by) boat
billete (m)	ticket
(en) camión (m)	(by) lorry
carretera (f) , camino (m)	road
(en) coche (m)	(by) car
conducir	to drive
(en) moto (f)	(by) motorbike
(en) tren (m)	(by) train

La comida – Food

La fruta	Fruit
cereza (f)	cherry
frambuesa (f)	raspberry
fresa (f)	strawberry
manzana (f)	apple
melocotón (m)	peach
naranja (f)	orange
pera (f)	pear
piña (f)	pineapple
plátano (m)	banana
uva (f)	grape

La verdura	Vegetables
guisantes (m pl)	peas
judías verdes (f pl)	green beans
patata (f)	potato
pepino (m)	cucumber
pimienta (f)	pepper
zanahoria (f)	carrot

General	General
carne (f)	meat
helado (m)	ice cream
huevo (m)	egg
jamón (m)	ham
marisco (m)	seafood
patatas fritas (f pl)	chips (warm) , crisps (packet)
pescado (m) (not *pez* for food)	fish
pollo (m)	chicken
queso (m)	cheese
sopa (f)	soup

Los empleos – Jobs

agente de policía (m)	police officer
amo de casa (m) / ama de casa (f)	house husband / house wife
camarero (m) / camarera (f)	waiter / waitress
carnicero (m) / carnicera (f)	butcher
cartero (m)	postman
conductor (m) / conductora (f) , chófer (m)	driver
dependiente (m) / dependienta (f)	shop assistant
director (m) / directora (f)	head teacher , manager
doctor (m) / doctora (f) , médico (m) / médica (f)	doctor
enfermero (m) / enfermera (f)	nurse
granjero (m) / granjera (f)	farmer
ingeniero (m) / ingeniera (f)	engineer
jefe (m)	boss
panadero (m) / panadera (f)	baker
peluquero (m) / peluquera (f)	hairdresser
profesor (m) / profesora (f) , maestro (m) / maestra (f)	teacher
secretario (m) / secretaria (f)	secretary
veterinario (m) / veterinaria (f)	vet

Note: In Spanish, you do **NOT** use *un* or *una* before the name of a job. For example:

- Mi madre es peluquera. – My mum is a hairdresser.
- Voy a hacerme médico en el futuro. – I am going to become a doctor in the future.

El medio ambiente – The Environment

agotar	to exhaust , to use up
ahorrar	to save
árbol (m)	tree
aumentar	to increase
barrio (m) , zona (f)	district , area
basura (f)	rubbish , garbage
bolsa de plástico (f)	plastic bag
botella de vidrio (f)	glass bottle
campo (m)	field
carril bici (m)	cycle lane
cartón (m)	cardboard
contaminación (f) , polución (f)	pollution
cultivar	to grow (crops)
deforestación (f)	deforestation
desechos (m pl) , desperdicios (m pl)	waste
desperdiciar , despilfarrar	to waste
efecto invernadero (m)	greenhouse effect
embalaje (m) , envase (m)	packaging , container
fábrica (f)	factory
incendio (m) , fuego (m)	fire
lata (f)	tin (can)
limpiar	to clean
mejorar	to improve
(centro de) reciclaje (m)	recycling (centre)
reciclar	to recycle
ruidoso	noisy
sucio	dirty
tráfico (m) , circulación (f)	traffic
transporte público (m)	public transport
zona peatonal (f)	pedestrian area

Amigos falsos

These Spanish words are similar to words in English, but actually mean something entirely different from their lookalikes. **Examiners love these!**

actual	current , present
actualmente	currently , at the moment
asistir	to attend , to be present
atender	to take care of
bizarro	brave
carpeta (f)	folder
carrera (f)	race , degree course
compromiso (m)	commitment , agreement , awkward situation
conductor (m) / conductora (f)	driver
contestar	to answer , to reply
cuestión (f)	matter , issue *(can be question too)*
decepción (f)	disappointment
delito (m)	crime
educado	polite
emocionante	exciting
excitante	sexually arousing
estar constipado / estar constipada	to have a cold
estar embarazada	to be pregnant
éxito (m)	success
fotógrafo (m)	photographer
gracioso	funny , cute
jubilación (f)	retirement
largo	long
lectura (f)	reading
librería (f)	bookshop , bookcase
mayor	older , larger , main
mermelada (f)	jam *(can be marmalade too)*
músico (m)	musician

nudo (m)	knot
pan (m)	bread
parientes (m pl)	relatives
patrón (m) / patrona (f)	boss , owner
pretender	to claim , to expect
real	royal *(can be real too)*
realizar	to fulfil , to carry out
recordar	to remember
ropa (f)	clothing
sensible	sensitive
soportar	to put up with, tolerate
suceso (m)	event , incident
suspender	to fail (exam)
últimamente	recently , lastly
último	last , final
vaso (m)	glass

Easily Confused Words

cansado	tired
casado	married
jabón (m)	soap
jamón (m)	ham
libre	free
libra (f)	pound (sterling)
libro (m)	book
llano	flat
lleno	full
llegar	to arrive
llenar	to fill
llevar	to wear , to carry
pero	but
perro (m)	dog
puerto (m)	port
puerta (f)	door

Cutting Out Grammar Errors

When you write in Spanish, you need to turn yourself into a computer that follows a series of steps to produce a word-by-word, grammatically correct sentence. Do this over and over again and you will have a number of grammatically correct sentences that form a grammatically correct essay. Simple.

The biggest hindrance to this is forgetfulness. Because we are used to talking in English without thinking about grammar, we naturally write in Spanish in a similar way. You translate words from English to Spanish in your head, and then write them down to form sentences. We have to override this natural flow of words to make our minds focus on the grammar involved. We must concentrate on each word to ensure we do not forget to make things grammatically correct. The sections which follow aim to give you the ability to cut out grammar errors... You just have to make sure you remember to follow the rules.

> **GOLDEN RULE :**
> **DON'T FORGET GRAMMAR**

Ohhh... and one more thing you have heard a couple of times before:

> **GOLDEN RULE :**
> **WRITE WHAT YOU KNOW, DON'T WRITE WHAT YOU**
> **DON'T KNOW**

Verbs

When studying languages, all students tend to hate verbs! They are the most important part of any language in order to boost your grade grammatically because the simple fact is: knowing how to use verbs instantly makes you stand out as a strong candidate. In reality, they are very straightforward. You merely need to know:

- Which tense to use
- How to form each tense according to:
  - Which tense you are using
  - Which person you are using from:

Person	Spanish	English	Example
1st Person Singular	*yo*	*I*	*I love football.*
2nd Person Singular	*tú*	*you* (singular)	*You own the house.*
3rd Person Singular	*él* **or** *ella* *usted* *'a noun'*	*he* **or** *she* **or** *it* *you* (formal singular) *'a noun'*	*Sharon hated that program.*
1st Person Plural	*nosotros* **or** *nosotras* *'1 or more nouns'* *y yo*	*we* *'1 or more nouns' and I*	*The dog and I went for a walk.*
2nd Person Plural	*vosotros* **or** *vosotras*	*you* (plural)	*You two have a huge house.*
3rd Person Plural	*ellos* **or** *ellas* *ustedes* *'2 or more nouns'*	*they* *you* (formal plural) *'2 or more nouns'*	*The bed and the table broke.*

> # GOLDEN RULE :
> ## IT IS NOT NECESSARY TO WRITE DOWN OR SAY THE PERSON YOU ARE USING
> In Spanish (as opposed to English and French), you do not need to directly express the person you are using. For example, if you are using the first person (i.e. *yo*), you simply need to use the correct verb conjugation. So, to say *I play*, you can just say *juego* (rather than *yo juego*). *Yo* is only used for emphasis (e.g. *Yo juego al fútbol mientras que mi hermano juega al tenis.*)
> However, if the person doing the action is not expressed by the verb's conjugation, you will need to write down or say the person (e.g. *mi hermano juega...* because *juega* does not express that my brother is playing).

What each tense means

First of all, let's look at what each tense is used for in Spanish along with examples (in English) of when it would be used.

Tenses	To...
Present	1) Say what you **normally** do.
	2) Describe the current state of affairs.
	E.g.1 *I **eat** fish all the time.*
	E.g.2 *I **think** that it **is** awful that there **are** so many wars.*
Present Progressive	Say what you are **currently** doing.
	E.g. *I **am trying** to do my homework but he **is distracting** me.*
Imperfect	1) Give a general description in the past (normally of a feeling or an opinion).
	2) Describe what you **used** to do.
	E.g.1 *He **felt** happy because it **was** exciting.*
	E.g.2 *I **used to** ride all the time.*

Preterite	Describe a completed action in the past. This is always used for something that someone did but has now stopped. E.g. *"Last night I only **drank** one beer, Mum!"*
Perfect	Say I *have never / always...* E.g. *I **have** never eaten paella but I **have** always wanted to.*
Pluperfect	Often describe something longer ago in the past than the perfect tense. It is used whenever in English you say I **had** + *past participle*. E.g. *Once I **had** finished eating, I went into town.*
Future (with *ir*)	Say what you **are going** to do in the immediate future. E.g. *Next week, I **am going** to buy a car.*
Future (without *ir*)	Say what you **will** do in the more distant future. E.g. *I **will** go to Las Vegas when I'm 21.*
Future Perfect	Say what you will have done in the future when (by the time) something else happens. E.g. *I **will have** eaten all the cake by the time mum gets back.*
Conditional	Portray something theoretical. It is used in English whenever you say I **would**... E.g. *I **would** try skydiving but I am too scared.*
Conditional Perfect	Portray something theoretical in the past. It is used in English whenever you say I **would have** + *past participle*. E.g. *I **would have** liked to have done it when I was younger, but now I am too old.*

Getting Rid of Verb Errors

The table we have just seen is probably a fairly scary one. There are 11 tenses included... "That is all far too difficult when you can barely work out how to use the present tense" is what many school teachers would tell you. This is a load of rubbish! In fact, the present, imperfect and preterite tenses are by far the hardest tenses to use and form, and if you have even the slightest grasp of these, using the other tenses really is easier. Trust me; the supposedly more difficult and complex tenses towards the end of the previous table - which will gain you **LOADS OF MARKS** - really are simple to form.

So, let's go through each tense and work out how to boost your **Accuracy** and **Use of language** marks by using each correctly.

Present Tense

Like I just said, the present tense is difficult. This is because there are so many irregulars and unfortunately the irregulars tend to be the most commonly used verbs.

However, first of all, you need to know how to form regular present tense verbs. All you need to do is to take the infinitive form of the verb (e.g. *tomar*, *comer*, *vivir*), remove the *-ar*, *-er*, *-ir* and then add the following endings:

	-ar	**-er**	**-ir**
1st person sg.	-o	-o	-o
2nd person sg.	-as	-es	-es
3rd person sg.	-a	-e	-e
1st person pl.	-amos	-emos	-imos
2nd person pl.	-áis	-éis	-ís
3rd person pl.	-an	-en	-en

The irregulars are harder to learn... In Spanish, there are two 'problem' types of verb:

1. **Radical Changing Verbs** (also known as **Stem Changing Verbs / Root Changing Verbs / Boot Verbs**) – Verbs that use the endings above, but whose stem is not simply the infinitive without the *-ar*, *-er* or *-ir*. Here, it is possible to learn the patterns of the verb stem changes as there are only a few.
2. **Irregular Verbs** – These simply have to be learnt individually.

Radical Changing Verbs

The first problem is that you need to remember that this change of stem **only** occurs in the **1ˢᵗ, 2ⁿᵈ, 3ʳᵈ person singular** and **3ʳᵈ person plural**. The second problem is that only some verbs containing certain letters change in a certain way; other verbs containing the same letters are regular verbs and don't change their stem at all. However, once you know these verb stem changes and which verbs they apply to, you simply add the regular verb endings to the correct stem. The majority of present tense stem changes involve the letters *o* and *e* in the infinitive changing to something else in the new present tense stem (1ˢᵗ, 2ⁿᵈ, 3ʳᵈ p.sg. & 3ʳᵈ p.pl):

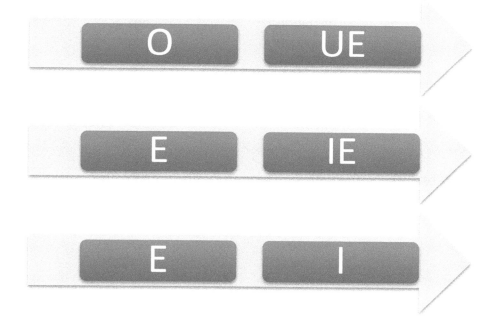

The only verb of importance that has a radical stem change and does not follow any of the above is *jugar*. Its present stem change is:

... So, which verbs actually adhere to these stem changes? Below is a table of the most commonly used radical changing verbs. I have also included the 1st person singular (I) form under the meaning of each verb in the table (as well as additional details for *llover*, which is only used in the 3rd person singular, and *elegir*, because it is an irregular, radical changing verb).

O ⟶ UE	E ⟶ IE	E ⟶ I
acostarse to go to bed me acuesto	**cerrar** to close cierro	**competir** to compete, to rival compito
contar (con) to narrate, count (on) cuento	**despertar** to wake up despierto	**conseguir** to get, to obtain consigo
dormir to sleep duermo	**empezar** to begin empiezo	**elegir** to choose elijo (I choose) eliges (you choose)
encontrar to find encuentro	**entender** to understand entiendo	elige (he / she chooses) eligen (they choose)
llover to rain llueve (it is raining)	**mentir** to lie miento	**medir** to measure mido
mostrar to show muestro	**pensar** to think pienso	**pedir** to ask for, to order pido
poder to be able puedo	**perder** to lose pierdo	**reír** to laugh río
probar to prove, test, taste pruebo	**preferir** to prefer prefiero	**repetir** to repeat repito
recordar to remember recuerdo	**querer** to want quiero	**seguir** to follow, to continue sigo
soñar (con) to dream (about) sueño	**sentirse** to feel me siento	**servir (para)** to serve, to be used (for) sirvo
volver to return vuelvo	**tender (a)** to tend (to) tiendo	**vestirse** to get dressed, to wear me visto

These verbs with this sort of stem change are also known as **boot verbs**. This is because (sorry to keep going on about it) the 1st and 2nd persons plural (*nosotros* and *vosotros*) **do not** change their stems like the rest of the verb. As you can see, the persons of the verb that **do** change their stem form the shape of a boot, hence the name *boot verbs*.

Irregular Verbs

Ideally, you would know every part of every irregular verb, but this is unrealistic and actually unnecessary to achieve a top grade. Instead, learn the 1st and 3rd person singular and the 1st person plural of 10 of the most common irregulars, and then make sure you use these in your essays. I do not include *haber* in that list because this needs to be learnt fully and we will see why in a minute!

Verb	1st Person Singular	3rd Person Singular	1st Person Plural
decir (to say)	digo	dice	decimos
estar (to be)	estoy	está	estamos
hacer (to do/make)	hago	hace	hacemos
ir (to go)	voy	va	vamos
poner (to put)	pongo	pone	ponemos
saber (to know)	sé	sabe	sabemos
salir (to go out)	salgo	sale	salimos
ser (to be)	soy	es	somos
tener (to have)	tengo	tiene	tenemos
venir (to come)	vengo	viene	venimos

So, those verbs are crucial to learn and use in your essays. There are also two golden saviours for you to employ when you are not certain of a verb's formation in the person you want to use. The first saviour is to use a present tense phrase (found on pg. 36), many of which simply require you to know the infinitive of the verb you want to use. The second saviours are verbs which are followed by an infinitive. The best ones to use are shown below:

	poder (to be able to)	deber (to have to)	querer (to want to)	gustar (to like)
1st person sg.	puedo	debo	quiero	me gusta
2nd person sg.	puedes	debes	quieres	te gusta
3rd person sg.	puede	debe	quiere	le gusta
1st person pl.	podemos	debemos	queremos	nos gusta
2nd person pl.	podéis	debéis	queréis	os gusta
3rd person pl.	pueden	deben	quieren	les gusta

So, if I wanted to say: *I go out with my friends every ten days*, but couldn't remember the parts of *salir* (which I should know!), I'd instead say: *I like to go out with my friends every ten days*.

Salgo *con mis amigos cada diez días. – I go out with my friends every ten days.*

Me gusta **salir** *con mis amigos cada diez días. – I like to go out with my friends every ten days.*

Present Progressive

This tense is formed using *estar [pr.p]*. It is the Spanish equivalent of the English: *to be [pr.p.]* (e.g. *estoy* **escribiendo** *– I am* **writing**). However, given its meaning as happening right now, you will not need to use it in your exam so I shall not cover it in any further detail.

Imperfect Tense

Fortunately for us, only three verbs are irregular in the imperfect: *ir*, *ser* and *ver*!
For all verbs except these three, you simply take the stem of the verb (the infinitive without -*ar*, -*er* or -*ir*) and add the following endings:

	-ar	-er & -ir
1st person sg.	-aba	-ía
2nd person sg.	-abas	-ías
3rd person sg.	-aba	-ía
1st person pl.	-ábamos	-íamos
2nd person pl.	-abais	-íais
3rd person pl.	-aban	-ían

Even more fortunately, despite their 'irregularity', the endings of the three irregulars are in fact very similar to, if not the same as, the endings above.

	ser	ir	ver
1st person sg.	era	iba	veía
2nd person sg.	eras	ibas	veías
3rd person sg.	era	iba	veía
1st person pl.	éramos	íbamos	veíamos
2nd person pl.	erais	ibais	veíais
3rd person pl.	eran	iban	veían

The hardest thing about the imperfect is knowing when to use it. If you want to show off your knowledge of forming and using it, the four easiest ways to do so are:

1. Use *era* meaning *it was* (from *ser*) along with an adjective to demonstrate your opinion of something. E.g. *La película que vimos ayer era fenomenal.*
2. Use *había* meaning *there was* or *there were.* (For more on *haber* constructions have a look at pg. 119.) E.g. *Ayer había un problema cuando llegamos al cine.*
3. Describe the weather in the past using *hacía...* E.g. *Fuimos al centro comercial porque hacía mal tiempo.*
4. Use an imperfect tense phrase (found on pg. 40). Of the phrases given in this section, a particularly useful one is the forth one:

Estaba [pr.p.]... cuando [preterite] – I was [pr.p.]... when [perfect]

Estaba buscando mis llaves cuando encontré mi bufanda. – I was looking for my keys when I found my scarf.

This is because it in fact uses another tense not yet mentioned: the **imperfect progressive**. Do not be scared of yet another tense as this is very similar to the present progressive (covered at the bottom of pg. 88), and translates directly to the English *I was [pr.p]*. It should only be used as in the phrase above to describe something that *was happening when* something else *happened.*

Using this phrase will certainly suggest a profound understanding of the imperfect tense to the examiner and is sure to gain you marks.

Preterite

In Spanish, the main tense used to describe past actions is the preterite. This is a crucial tense to learn if you want to succeed in your Spanish exam. It is also the trickiest because (you guessed it!) there are the most irregulars. The only saviour to these irregulars is that some of them have patterns in common which makes them a bit easier to learn. Regular verbs are formed in exactly the same manner as every other tense we have seen: take the stem and add the endings. The stem for the preterite for regular verbs is the infinitive with *-ar*, *-er* or *-ir* removed. The regular endings of the preterite are below:

	-ar	-er & -ir
1st person sg.	-é	-í
2nd person sg.	-aste	-iste
3rd person sg.	-ó	-ió
1st person pl.	-amos	-imos
2nd person pl.	-asteis	-isteis
3rd person pl.	-aron	-ieron

So, let's move on to the irregulars. I would advise that you just bite the bullet and spend a good few hours over the course of a few days learning these irregulars until you know them well. I'm afraid this is one of the few areas in which I can offer very little assistance or any way of speeding up the process.

I have grouped these irregular verbs such that those in the same tone of blue shading in the same table have similar patterns of formation; this should hopefully make them easier to learn. It is crucial that you spend some time memorising these if you want to obtain a top grade.

Tip: You will notice that none of the irregular verbs in the preterite has an accent. Therefore, if you know a verb is irregular, this is one less aspect to worry about!

	ser	ir	tener	estar
1st person sg.	fui	fui	tuve	estuve
2nd person sg.	fuiste	fuiste	tuviste	estuviste
3rd person sg.	fue	fue	tuvo	estuvo
1st person pl.	fuimos	fuimos	tuvimos	estuvimos
2nd person pl.	fuisteis	fuisteis	tuvisteis	estuvisteis
3rd person pl.	fueron	fueron	tuvieron	estuvieron

Note: The verbs *ser* and *ir* both have the same form throughout the preterite. Therefore, if you come across them, you will have to work out the meaning of the verb from the context in which you find it. E.g. *fuimos a la playa* could mean either *we went to the beach* or *we were to the beach*. Evidently *fuimos* here is from *ir* not *ser* as only the first translation makes sense.

	decir	conducir	poder	poner
1st person sg.	dije	conduje	pude	puse
2nd person sg.	dijiste	condujiste	pudiste	pusiste
3rd person sg.	dijo	condujo	pudo	puso
1st person pl.	dijimos	condujimos	pudimos	pusimos
2nd person pl.	dijisteis	condujisteis	pudisteis	pusisteis
3rd person pl.	dijeron	condujeron	pudieron	pusieron

	venir	ver	dar	hacer	querer
1st person sg.	vine	vi	di	hice	quise
2nd person sg.	viniste	viste	diste	hiciste	quisiste
3rd person sg.	vino	vio	dio	hizo	quiso
1st person pl.	vinimos	vimos	dimos	hicimos	quisimos
2nd person pl.	vinisteis	visteis	disteis	hicisteis	quisisteis
3rd person pl.	vinieron	vieron	dieron	hicieron	quisieron

Future (without *ir*) & Conditional Tenses

These two tenses are formed in a very similar and easy way. Unfortunately, there are irregulars to learn. However, they aren't too difficult as the only part that is irregular is the stem; the endings are always the same. Another positive is that you already know the conditional endings because they are exactly the same as the imperfect ones for *-er* and *-ir* verbs (covered on pg. 89). Even better, for regular verbs the future and conditional stem is simply the **infinitive**. Then, you simply add the *-er* and *-ir* imperfect endings to form the conditional (given as a reminder below), and the following endings to form the future:

Person	Future Ending	Conditional Ending
1st sg.	-é	-ía
2nd sg.	-ás	-ías
3rd sg.	-á	-ía
1st pl.	-emos	-íamos
2nd pl.	-éis	-íais
3rd pl.	-án	-ían

Here are the most common irregular verbs in the future and conditional tenses:

Verb	Stem	1st Person Singular Future	1st Person Singular Conditional
decir (to say)	dir-	diré	diría
hacer (to do/make)	har-	haré	haría
poder (to be able to)	podr-	podré	podría
poner (to put)	pondr-	pondré	pondría
querer (to want)	querr-	querré	querría
saber (to know)	sabr-	sabré	sabría
salir (to go out)	saldr-	saldré	saldría
tener (to have)	tendr-	tendré	tendría
venir (to come)	vendr-	vendré	vendría

Future Tense (with *ir*)

This is extremely easy to form and is comparable to saying *I am going to...* in English. You simply use the correct part of the present tense of *ir*, followed by *a* and an infinitive.

Part of *ir* + *a* + Infinitive

E.g. Voy a ir al centro comercial hoy. Mi padre va a venir conmigo. Vamos a hacer compras.

This is a great way to use the future tense, particularly in an oral, if you forget an irregular future stem or just panic and forget a future ending. However, be wary! Examiners will want to see the use of the future tense (without *ir*), which we have just covered, in your essay or during your oral. Therefore, it is important that you show the examiner you are capable of using **both** forms of the future tense in order to achieve the highest possible mark.

Tip: The future without *ir* and the future with *ir* are used pretty much interchangeably in Spanish, just like saying *I will* and *I'm going to* in English. They have slightly different meanings, so in English it sounds slightly unnatural to say: *I will leave this Tuesday*. Instead, you'd say: *I'm going to leave this Tuesday*. However, you certainly will not be marked down for using one instead of the other in terms of their meaning... But, bear in mind what I have just said about needing to use the future without *ir*.

Perfect, Pluperfect, Future Perfect & Conditional Perfect

Now we are coming towards what are generally considered the 'very difficult' and 'advanced' tenses. However, these four tenses are all formed in a very similar way. Rather than having just one word, like most other tenses we have seen so far, these four tenses are composed of two words.

Part of *haber* + Past Participle

E.g.   **he**   **comido**

To form these four compound tenses, you simply need to use a different tense of *haber* (and we have already covered each of these four tenses)! So, which tense of *haber* do you need to use for each compound tense?

Compound Tense	Tense of *haber*	Meaning
Perfect	Present	*has*
Pluperfect	Imperfect	*had*
Future Perfect	Future	*will have*
Conditional Perfect	Conditional	*would have*

Therefore, *haber* is probably the most important verb to know if you want to boost your (I)GCSE Spanish grade. You need to know **all six parts** of this crucial verb in the **present**, **imperfect, future** and **conditional** like you know how to spell your name (hopefully!). It is so important.

GOLDEN RULE :
LEARN *HABER*

---

haber

	present	imperfect	future	conditional
1st person sg.	he	había	habré	habría
2nd person sg.	has	habías	habrás	habrías
3rd person sg.	ha	había	habrá	habría
1st person pl.	hemos	habíamos	habremos	habríamos
2nd person pl.	habéis	habíais	habréis	habríais
3rd person pl.	han	habían	habrán	habrían

Note: If you look up the conjugation of *haber* (as given above), you will see that the 3rd person singular in the present tense also has the option *hay*. This is known as the impersonal form. This is there simply because *haber* has **two** uses:

1. In compound tenses (as it would be used here)
2. To mean *there is* or *there are*

It is in the second case that you would use *hay* instead of *ha*. More on this can be found on pg. 119.

So, now we have the part of *haber* sorted, what about the past participle? Back on pg. 97, we saw the example: *he comido*. If we look at this sentence grammatically, *comido* is a past participle. In English, most past participles end in *-ed* or *-en*. E.g. played (*jugado*), finished (*terminado*), driven (*conducido*), eaten (*comido*). However, there are plenty of irregulars. E.g. done (*hecho*), put (*puesto*), gone (*ido*). Fortunately for you, past participles are used in Spanish in exactly the same way as in English. Slightly less fortunately, there are quite a few irregulars you need to learn!

How to form a Past Participle

For the majority of verbs in Spanish, the past participle is formed by:

Infinitive Ending	Remove	Add	Example
-ar	ar	ado	*tocar* has past participle *tocado*
-er	er	ido	*tener* has past participle *tenido*
-ir	ir	ido	*subir* has past participle *subido*

Irregulars

Verb	Past Participle
abrir (to open)	abierto
decir (to say)	dicho
escribir (to write)	escrito
hacer (to do/make)	hecho
morir (to die)	muerto
poner (to put)	puesto
romper (to break)	roto
ver (to see)	visto
volver (to return)	vuelto

Tip: You should try and fit at least one of these irregular past participles into your essay as it is very impressive to an examiner. Maybe come up with a fairly generic set-phrase of your own that you can use in virtually any essay. E.g. *Nunca había visto algo así antes. – I had never seen anything like it before.*

Examples of the Perfect, Pluperfect, Future Perfect & Conditional Perfect

Just to give you an idea of how you might use these tenses in an essay, here are some sample sentences.

Note: There are also some phrases starting on pg. 41 containing all of these tenses, but I'm hoping once you understand the grammar, you will be able to make your own ones up too.

Perfect: Siempre **me ha gustado** nadar y por eso fui a la piscina con mi hermana. Sin embargo nuestro hermano no vino puesto que nunca **ha aprendido** a nadar. – **I have** always **liked** swimming and so I went to the pool with my sister. However, our brother did not come because **he has** never **learnt** to swim.

Pluperfect: Cuando **había llegado** a la casa de mi amigo y cuando él **había terminado** sus deberes, decidimos ver una película. – When **I had arrived** at my friend's house and when **he had finished** his homework, we decided to watch a film.

Future Perfect: A la edad de treinta años, **habré comprado** una casa muy grande. – When I am thirty, **I will have bought** a very big house.

Conditional Perfect: **Habría muerto** si no hubiera puesto mi cinturón de seguridad. – **I would have died** if I had not put on my seat belt.

Reflexives

Reflexive verbs involve someone doing something to himself / herself. Most of the reflexive verbs that you are likely to come across are to do with your daily routine. So, for example, *me levanto* translates literally to *I get **myself** up*, although in English the reflexive pronoun (myself) is often left out. What is a reflexive pronoun? It is an extra part that you have to add before all reflexive verbs, which otherwise behave in the same way as non-reflexive verbs.

So what are the reflexive pronouns?

Person	Reflexive Pronoun
1st sg.	me
2nd sg.	te
3rd sg.	se
1st pl.	nos
2nd pl.	os
3rd pl.	se

E.g. *Me despierto – I wake up*   *Se ducha – He showers*

There is only one other complication that you need to be aware of when it comes to reflexive verbs. If you use a verb or an expression that requires an infinitive, and you want to use a reflexive verb, you must remember to change the infinitive form to agree with the person you are describing. E.g. *Suelo levantar**me**... – I normally get up...* As shown in this example, the extra part always goes at the end of the infinitive. As a general rule, this is also the same for present participles; although technically the extra part can go before the first verb or at the end of the participle, the latter is much more common. E.g. *Estoy duchándo**me** – I am showering* has the extra part at the end of *duchando*. Also notice that the present participle takes an accent on the third to last vowel if it has a reflexive pronoun at the end.

Adjectives

Adjectives are words which describe nouns. In Spanish, unlike in English, they nearly always go after the noun they describe. So, in English we say *the small boy*, but in Spanish you must say *the boy small*, which translates to *el chico pequeño*.

Adjectives that go Before the Noun

There are a few exceptions to this, although the use of adjectives before nouns is relatively complicated and generally quite subtle so I won't go into too much detail on this. Adjectives that precede nouns have all sorts of uses in Spanish, but the most common ones that need to be learnt are given below. These **always** precede the noun, so should be learnt in order to avoid seeming like a lower standard candidate. There is a slight complication with some adjectives that go before the noun rather than after it: they lose their final -*o* when they precede a masculine singular noun.

Adjective	Masculine Singular	Feminine Singular	Masculine Plural	Feminine Plural
alguno	algún	alguna	algunos	algunas
mucho	mucho	mucha	muchos	muchas
ninguno	ningún	ninguna	*no plural form*	
poco	poco	poca	pocos	pocas
primero	primer	primera	primeros	primeras
tercero	tercer	tercera	terceros	terceras

*E.g. En **primer** lugar, quiero informarte que hay **pocos** libros en la biblioteca porque **mucha** gente los roba.*

In addition, *bueno*, *malo* and *grande* can appear both before and after the noun they describe. The positioning of these adjectives in a particular context is a complexity that you don't really need to worry about. If in doubt using these adjectives, just position them **after** the noun they describe, as you would with any other adjective. However, it is possible that you will come across these adjectives preceding a masculine singular noun, in which case you should be aware that they change to: **buen**, **mal** and **gran** respectively. Also note that *grande* after a noun means *big*, whereas *gran(de)* before a noun means *great*.

Agreement

To boost your grade, the most crucial aspect to understand concerning adjectives is agreement. So many students seem to panic when they hear that 'dreaded' word. This really is not difficult... It is far easier than what we have just covered in the *Verbs* section. Essentially, when you learn adjectives, they are given in the masculine singular form. If a noun is feminine or plural or both, you need to change this form. There are three types of adjectives, and their changes are very simple:

Adjectives ending in *-o*

	Masculine	Feminine
Singular	-o *el juego divertido*	-a *la mujer divertida*
Plural	-os *los juegos divertidos*	-as *las mujeres divertidas*

Adjectives ending in -e

	Masculine	Feminine
Singular	-e *el libro interesante*	-e *la noticia interesante*
Plural	-es *los libros interesantes*	-es *las noticias interesantes*

Adjectives ending in a consonant

	Masculine	Feminine
Singular	no change *el chico popular*	no change *la chica popular*
Plural	-es *los chicos populares*	-es *las chicas populares*

There are, like all things in languages, irregulars. However, in Spanish there are, in fact, only a very few minor irregularities. However, the following are relatively commonly used:

- Adjectives ending in *-ista*:

	Masculine	**Feminine**
Singular	-ista *el profesor idealista*	-ista *la profesora idealista*
Plural	-istas *los profesores idealistas*	-istas *las profesoras idealistas*

- *feli**z*** changes to *feli**ces*** in the plural
  *El hombre es feli**z**.*
  *Los hombres son feli**ces**.*
- *j**o**ven* takes an accent on the *o* in the plural: *j**ó**venes*
  *La mujer j**o**ven no tiene mucho dinero.*
  *Las mujeres j**ó**venes no tienen mucho dinero.*
- *inglés* (meaning *English*) changes to *ingles**a*** in the feminine singular, *inglés* in the masculine plural and *ingles**as*** in the feminine plural
  Mi hijo es inglés.
  *Mi hija es ingles**a**.*
  Mis hijos son inglés.
  *Mis hijas son ingles**as**.*
  Many adjectives of nationality follow a similar pattern to this.

Don't worry too much about these slight irregularities; if you make a small mistake in the use of an irregular adjective, you **will not** be heavily penalised. However, if you make mistakes with basic regular agreement you **will** be penalised.

Often, people don't drop marks in their exams because they don't know how to make regular adjectives agree, but because they forget to make them agree. This is because we don't do it in English. So, look at the checking rules for every time you write in Spanish - Part 2 on pg. 58 applies to making sure adjectives agree. However, first and foremost, make sure you remember the Golden Rule and don't forget grammar!

Nouns

All you really need to be able to do concerning nouns in Spanish to boost your grade is tell what gender (masculine or feminine) a noun is and be able to put it into the plural. You need to be able to tell the gender of a noun so that you use the correct version of *the* (i.e. *el*, *la*, *los* or *las*) and also so that you can make any adjective that may accompany that noun agree (as we have just seen).

The first thing to note is that if you are given a noun in a reading comprehension or an essay title, do not then use it in an answer or an essay in the wrong gender. This just shows you are careless and gives an examiner completely the wrong impression. There was an example of this in a mock paper I did, in which 11 out of 28 people who took the mock did the following:

Question: En **la foto** que describe Eduardo ¿qué hacen los niños?

Response: En **el foto** que describe Eduardo...

So, over a third of my class were incapable of copying the gender of *foto* correctly on the line below the question. This is madness and will probably lose you a mark!

GOLDEN RULE :
DON'T GET NOUN GENDERS WRONG IF YOU ARE GIVEN THEM

So, aside from that, when you want to use a noun, you need to be able to try and deduce what gender it is. So, here is a pretty comprehensive guide to working out the gender of a word which will work the vast majority of the time.

The Rules of Sex

In Spanish (fortunately for you), working out the gender of a noun is usually pretty straightforward. This is because, in Spanish (most of the time), if a noun ends in -*o*, it is masculine; if a noun ends in -*a*, it is feminine. Simple. There are a few exceptions to this rule (such as *la foto* as we saw in the example on the previous page):

Feminine ending in -*o*
la foto
la mano
la moto
la radio

Masculine ending in -*a*
el cli**ma**
el dra**ma**
el idio**ma**
el proble**ma**
el progra**ma**
el siste**ma**
el te**ma**
el día
el mapa
el planeta

Note: You may have noticed that many of the masculine words ending in -*a* end in -*ma*.

It is also important to note that very occasionally a word beginning with *a*- or *ha*- will be preceded by *el* rather than *la*, even though it is feminine. The two most important examples of this are: *el agua* and *el hambre*. This use of *el* is purely for ease of speech (as opposed to *la agua*) and does not make *agua* or *hambre* masculine. Therefore, *the cold water* translates to *el agua fría*.

Then, we must consider nouns that do not end in -*o* or -*a*. These are far more difficult to categorise into masculine and feminine, although there are a few endings to look out for as being feminine:

Ending	Example(s)	Exception(s)
-ión	la televisión	el avión
-dad	la calidad	
-tad	la amistad	
-tud	la juventud	
-z	la actriz, la paz, la luz	el lápiz, el arroz, el pez

Nouns ending in consonants, except those in the table on the previous page, are nearly all masculine (e.g. *el árbol*). Then, the only noun ending left is *-e*. This is the trickiest but, for the most part, a noun ending in *-e* is masculine unless it is one of the following:

la calle	la gente	la noche
la carne	la llave	la nube
la clase	la madre	la sangre
la frase	la muerte	la suerte
la fuente	la nieve	la tarde

Gender Checker

Plural Nouns

So, how do you make a noun plural? If the noun ends in *-o*, *-a* or *-e*, you add an *-s* to the end (e.g. *los chicos*). If it ends in a consonant you add *-es* (e.g. *los colores*). Also be aware that nouns ending *-ión* drop the accent in the plural (e.g. *la sección*, *las secciones*) and nouns ending in *-z* add *-es* and also change the *-z* to *-c* (e.g. *la voz*, *las voces*).

Ser & Estar

This is one of the most difficult aspects of the Spanish language and is something that all native English speakers struggle with. The simple fact is that you will make mistakes, but I hope to give you a better sense of when you should use each of *ser* and *estar*. I am not going to give you a long list of intricate rules or complex acronyms because, all too often, these rules don't work or cause you to over-think the difference between these two verbs. Instead, I hope to give you a better overview of when the two verbs are used and to clarify their slightly different meanings.

Ser (=)

Ser is like an equals sign. This equals sign tends to denote a fixed identity or a defining characteristic, normally less disputable and of a more permanent nature.

- *Ser* is used to show A = B, where both A and B are nouns. This is always the case: *estar* cannot be used to say that two nouns are equivalent.
  E.g. *Barcelona es un equipo español.*
     Tom es un chico guapo.
     Lynne es mi madre.

- *Ser* is also used with adverbs of time which cause one of the two nouns in an identity (A = B) to be omitted, but where that noun could be reintroduced to give the same meaning. For example, *hoy es miércoles* is equivalent to *hoy (**el día**) es **miércoles*** (A = B) with *el día* omitted.
  E.g. *Ayer fue mi cumpleaños. = Ayer (**el día**) fue **mi cumpleaños**.*
     *Ahora son las cinco. = Ahora (**las horas**) son **las cinco**.*

Note: Time is an important use of *ser* to point out. This is because students are often confused by the idea of permanence. Surely there is nothing less permanent than time? Within a minute, the statement *ahora son las cinco* will be incorrect. Yet, you must use *son las cinco* rather than *están...* because really you are saying: *The time is five o'clock*. This statement is an identity between two nouns, so *ser* must be used. Also, when giving the time, remember to use **es** *la una* for *it's one o'clock* and **son** *las...* for all other hours. Turn to pg. 114 for more information.

- Phrases detailing occupation also require the use of *ser*.
  E.g. *Ellos son estudiantes.*
     Mi padre era jardinero.

Note: Occupation is another case where students are often confused by permanence. You don't have to be a student or a gardener forever, so surely *estar* would be more appropriate? As true as that is, here we are again using A = B, and here the statements are wholly indisputable: you either are or are not a student or a gardener.

- Similarly, *ser* is used when using adjectives that describe permanent identity or nature, such as the place of origin of a person or the material from which something is made. Here, the notion of *ser* as '=' is most clear because these identities do not change.
  E.g. *Tom es de Inglaterra.*
     Julia es española.
     La mesa es de madera.

Ser **is used to give either a physical or characteristic description of someone or something in comparison with others (as opposed to in comparison with the *normal* state of that same person or object).**

 comparison with others

E.g. *Mi hermano es alto, moreno y delgado.*
   Su pelo es largo y rubio.
   Mi novio es romántico y cariñoso.
   Zara es inteligente y poderosa.

Note: Clearly you can grow or become fatter or cut your hair or become more romantic. Therefore, the notions of permanence or of something as indisputable are even less applicable here. The key idea is that of description in comparison with others.

Ser is used to denote possession.

E.g. *El bolígrafo es de Juan.*
Todo esto es mío pero el día de mañana será tuyo.

Ser is only ever used to denote location when describing an event (when *to be* means *to be held* or *to happen*).

E.g. *La fiesta es en la casa de Sam.*
¿Dónde fue el accidente?

Estar (≈)

Estar is like 'approximately equal to', or 'temporarily equal to'. It tends not to denote permanent identity or defining characteristics, but instead short-term state, circumstance or emotion.

- *Estar* is used to express emotion or condition that would not be seen as a characteristic feature, but instead as a temporary state or feeling.
  E.g. *Los platos están sucios.*
  El niño está enfermo hoy.
  Estoy muy cansado porque trabajé muy duro ayer.
  Mi padre está contento esta semana.

Note: There are a few words that don't adhere to this. The following must be used with *ser*: *feliz, desgraciado, pobre, rico* (*rich*), *culpable, inocente*.

- *Estar* is also used with adverbs, except for with adverbs of time (see the second bullet point on pg. 108). An adverb is a word that describes a verb (most adverbs in English end in *-ly* e.g. *quickly*). I think it is easiest to see why *estar* is used with adverbs by considering adverbs as describing a temporary way in which something happens.
  E.g. *El viento está fuerte hoy. Normalmente está débil aquí.*
  Mi hermano está bien después de recuperarse de la operación.

- Similarly, *estar de* is used to depict temporary mood or situation.
  E.g. *Están de buen humor.*
  Mi amigo está de viaje en España.

Estar is used to give either a physical or characteristic description of someone or something in comparison with the *normal* state of that same person or object.

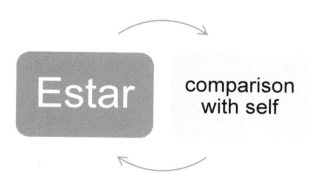

E.g. *Pienso que hoy estás tonto porque no dormiste bien anoche.*
Sara hoy está más guapa que nunca.

Estar is used to give information about location, position or posture.

- The usage of *estar* to depict position or posture is in line with the notion of temporary state.
E.g. *Mi madre está sentada.*
Pablo estaba en el centro comercial cuando cayó.

- However, the use of *estar* to denote location seems strange as the location of some things is evidently permanent (e.g. *the beach is next to the sea*). This is just about the only occasion with respect to *ser* and *estar* when I shall simply tell you to remember the rule: **location requires the use of *estar*, unless an <u>event's</u> location is in question, in which case *ser* must be used.**

Estar is used with ongoing actions using the present progressive tense.

E.g. *Estoy escribiendo una redacción.*

Note: In Spanish, death is considered as an ongoing action rather than a permanent state, thus *estar*, rather than *ser*, is used with *muerto*. E.g. *Mi abuela está muerta.*

Changes in Meaning with *Ser* & *Estar*

Adjective	Meaning with *Ser*	Meaning with *Estar*
aburrido	boring	bored
bueno	good	tasty , attractive
cansado	tiresome	tired
interesado	self-seeking	interested
listo	clever	ready
malo	bad	ill
orgulloso	vain , arrogant	proud
pesado	heavy	dull , boring
rico	rich	tasty
seguro	safe	certain
verde	green	unripe
vivo	sharp , alert	alive

Tips and Tricks – Golden Nuggets to Remember

Nugget	Examples
Ir de vacaciones There are two points to make here: 1. The word *vacaciones* (holiday(s)) is never singular. In Spanish, you must say *I went on holidays* **NOT** *I went on holiday.* 2. *de* cannot be replaced with anything else. The phrase *fui en vacaciones* means nothing in Spanish.	El año pasado fui de vacaciones. **NOT** El año pasado fui de vacación. **NOR** El año pasado fui en vacaciones.

Por & Para

These two words are two of the trickiest words in the Spanish language. Knowing when to use each of them is sometimes confusing for the most fluent Spanish speakers. Therefore, don't worry about trying to learn all of their uses. Instead, become familiar with their most common applications listed below:

Por

Por	Examples

1. Period of time
2. Meaning *through* or *along*
3. Meaning *by* with communication, transportation
4. *Por la mañana / tarde / noche*
5. Expressions:
    a. por ciento – percent
    b. por cierto – certainly
    c. por ejemplo – for example
    d. por eso – therefore
    e. por favor – please
    f. por primera vez – for the first time
    g. por supesto – of course
    h. por todas partes – everywhere
	1. Estudié por cuatro horas.
	2. Caminé por la calle.
	3. Me gusta viajar por tren y hablar por teléfono.
	4. *See next golden nugget*

Para

1. Meaning *in order to*

2. Purpose
3. *Para mí / ti etc.* expressing recipient or opinion

> **Note:** *Para mí* has an accent on the *'i'* when it is used to mean *for me*. However, *for my sister* is *para mi hermana* (no accent). *Para ti* does not have an accent either.

Examples

1. Para tener éxito, debes trabajar duro y concentrarte.
2. El vaso es para agua.
3. El regalo es para ti.
   Para mí, lo más importante es mantenerme en forma.

Por la mañana / tarde / noche

If you want to say *in the morning, I went...* you must say *por la mañana fui... NOT en la mañana fui...*

However, *en* can be used to mean *in* with months, seasons and years. To say *I'll be leaving in July*, you say *Me iré en Julio NOT Me iré por Julio.*

> **Note:** You can use *de la mañana* in the sense of *at 4 o'clock in the morning – a las cuatro de la mañana*.

Por la mañana siempre me levanto a las siete. **NOT En** la mañana siempre me levanto a las siete.

Terminaré mi libro **en** el verano porque tendré mucho tiempo libre. **NOT** Terminaré mi libro **por** el verano porque tendré mucho tiempo libre.

Mañana **por** la mañana compraré un coche caro. **NOT** Mañana **en** la mañana compraré un coche caro.

> **Note:** *Mañana* also means *tomorrow*.

Time

In Spanish, giving a time is slightly trickier than in English. For a start, any time must always include either *la* or *las*: *la* for any time including the word *una* (one o'clock) and *las* for all other times. Secondly, to say *it is...* you must use *es* for any time including *una* and *son* for all other times.

Es la una menos cuarto.

Son las tres y media.

Fui al banco a las diez de la mañana.

Comeremos a la una y cuarto.

Days of the Week

On *Sunday* cannot be translated literally into Spanish. (This of course applies for all days of the week, not just Sunday!) In fact, *on Sunday* has two distinct translations with two different meanings:

1. *El domingo* means on one particular Sunday.
2. *Los domingos* means on Sunday in general (i.e. every Sunday).

El lunes decidimos ir a la bolera ya que llovía todo el día.

Los jueves trato de ir a la planta de reciclado de vidrio.

Los fines de semana suelo jugar al fútbol con mis hermanos.

Estar bien NOT *Ser bien*

Ser can (almost) never precede an adverb. The cases when it can are very rare so assume this is always the rule.

Estoy bien hoy. **NOT** Soy bien hoy.

Jugar & Tocar

In Spanish, there are two words for *to play*. *Jugar* is used for sports, while *tocar* is used for music (and also means *to touch*).

Mi mejor amigo juega al baloncesto pero yo prefiero tocar el violín.

CAROLINA

Carolina contains all of the consonants in the Spanish language that can appear as a double (i.e. *cc*, *rr*, *ll* and *nn* are the only double consonants).

cc : a**cc**ión, dire**cc**ión

rr : pe**rr**o, ce**rr**ar

ll : **ll**ave, po**ll**o

nn : co**nn**otar, i**nn**ato

Lo NOT *La Cosa*

La cosa translates literally to *the thing*. However, this *thing* is a physical thing that you can touch. For example, *la cosa que está en la mesa* – the thing that is on the table. When describing a concept, you must instead use *lo*. For example, *lo más preocupante es que nunca va al colegio* – the most worrying thing is that he never goes to school.

En mi opinión, **lo serio** es que no hemos solucionado la crisis económica. **NOT** En mi opinión, **la cosa seria** es que no hemos solucionado la crisis económica.

Para mí, **lo que** no soporto es la pereza. **NOT** Para mí, **la cosa que** no soporto es la pereza.

Pero & Sino

In Spanish, *but* can be translated in two different ways: *pero* and *sino*. *Sino* is only used in one very specific case: when one idea is rejected *but* another is accepted without the introduction of another verb. In all other cases, *pero* is used.

No me gusta la bufanda **sino** la corbata. – I don't like the scarf but (I do like) the tie.

No quiero ir a Barcelona **pero** la arquitectura de Gaudí me interesa. – I don't want to go to Barcelona but Gaudi's architecture does interest me.

en or a

In Spanish, there is often confusion over when to use *en* and when to use *a*. In fact, the rules are very simple: if you're moving *to* a place, you use *a*; if you're not moving, you use *en*.

A very common mistake is to translate literally from the English. For example, *I am at the supermarket – Estoy al supermercado*. This is incorrect because you are not moving *to* the supermarket. You are already there, so must use *en*: *Estoy en el supermercado*.

This rule also applies to countries and towns (very differently from in French if you also study that). If you're going to it's *a*, if you're there it's *en*.

Me encanta ir **a** España porque hace mucho calor.

No me gusta nada quedarme **en** hoteles **en** España, sobre todo cuando voy **a** Barcelona, porque están sucios.

Cuando tenga dieciocho años, me gustaría vivir **en** China porque siempre he soñado con ir **a** Beijing.

Personal *a*

Another case of students making silly grammatical errors is in the use of the personal a. Again, the rule as for when to use it is very simple, but - because we do not have an equivalent in English - people forget it all too often.

Every time you use a person or group of people as the object of a verb (i.e. every time a person or group of people is having something done to them), you must remember to put in an *a* before the object.

Conozco **a** mucha gente rica. **NOT** Conozco mucha gente rica.

Oigo **a** Ola porque tiene una voz ruidosa. **NOT** Oigo Ola porque tiene una voz ruidosa.

Jaime no reconoció **a** su propia madre. **NOT** Jaime no reconoció su propia madre.

Menos

This word has the potential to lose you marks because, depending on the way it is used, it can mean two entirely opposite things.

It is quite often used in reading or listening exercises to try and trick you, so watch out for it!

por lo menos... or *al menos...* means *at least...*

menos de... means *less than...* (followed by a number)

menos que... means *less than...* (or *not as much as*)

En España hay **por lo menos / al menos** treinta millones de coches. – In Spain, there are **at least** thirty million cars.

En España hay **menos de** treinta millones de coches. – In Spain there are **less than** thirty million cars.

Mi madre comió **menos que** mi padre. – My mum ate **less than** my dad.

Todo el mundo

When using *todo el mundo* to mean *everyone* or when using other groups of people using *todo* or *toda* (e.g. *toda la familia*), you must remember that this is a **singular** group of people. There may be more than one person, but there is only one group. Therefore, any verb which follows this must be in the 3rd person **singular NOT plural**. Also, any adjectives which agree must be in the **singular NOT plural**. This also applies for *la gente*, very commonly used in Spanish to mean *people (in general)*.

Todo el mundo sueñ**a** con tener mucho dinero. **NOT** Todo el mundo sueñ**an** con tener mucho dinero.

Tod**a** mi familia est**aba** content**a**. **NOT** Tod**a** mi familia est**aban** content**as**.

Hay much**a** gente que se preocup**a** por las apariencias. **NOT** Hay much**as** gente que se preocup**an** por las apariencias.

Present + *desde hace*

In English, we say **I have been doing** something for 5 years. Therefore, students often translate this using perfect + *desde hace...* However, in Spanish, you must use the present instead of the perfect.

If you really want to impress the examiner, maybe use the construction *llevo X años [pr.p]*.

Juego al golf desde hace diez años. – I have been playing golf for ten years.

Llevo **siete** años **viviendo** en Londres. – I have been living in London for 7 years.

Se

This little word can be placed before the 3rd person singular of any verb in order to change its meaning. It is extremely common in Spanish and has two uses:

1. To mean *you (generally)* – to make an overarching point about something.
   For example, *you shouldn't eat too much sugar.*
2. To give something a passive meaning. This is actually very similar to the first usage, but just translates slightly differently to English.
   For example, *sugar shouldn't be eaten too much.*

The two examples given above would both be translations of the same sentence: *no se debería comer demasiado azúcar.* Here, the first translation sounds far more natural in English. However, there are cases when the passive voice sounds more natural. For example, *se sabe que mucha gente come demasiado azúcar.* Here, the two posible translations are:

1. *You (generally) know that lots of people eat too much sugar.*
2. *It is known that lots of people eat too much sugar.*

Clearly the second translation is better here.

No se puede negar que la obesidad es un problema grave hoy en día. – You cannot deny that obesity is a serious problem nowadays.

Se piensa que un treinta por ciento de la población inglesa tiene una mascota. – It is thought that thirty percent of the English population have a pet.

Es imprescindible que se considere todas las opciones. – It is essential that you consider all of the options. **OR** It is essential that all of the options are considered.

Pronounce *'V'* like *'B'*

In Spanish, the letter '*v*' should be pronounced like the English letter '*b*'.

vamos is pronounced *bamos*

Lots of *haber*

In Spanish, *haber* (as well as being used in compound tenses) means *there is* or *there are*. **It does not change in the plural.** There are lots of different forms of *haber* that can be used in your essays to show off your knowledge of tenses.

hay – there is / are

había – there was / were (on going)

hubo – there was / were (completed)

ha habido – there has / have been

había habido – there had been

habrá – there will be

habría – there would be

habrá habido – there will have been

habría habido – there would have been

debe haber – there must be

debería haber – there should be

habría debido haber – there should have been

podría haber – there could be

habría podido haber – there could have been

Note: See pg. 81-82 and pg. 89-93 on when to use the imperfect or preterite.

The Golden Rules

WRITING EXAM

1. Write what you know, don't write what you don't know
2. Don't write too much - there is a word limit for a reason
3. Use phrases but don't force them - if a sentence sounds unnatural, you will lose marks

ORAL EXAM

4. Say what you know, don't say what you don't know
5. Be prepared but sound spontaneous - use what you have learnt while sounding chatty
6. Expand your answers - give as much detail as possible with reasons and opinions included
7. Breathe slowly and remember: everyone is nervous before their oral!

CONTROLLED ASSESSMENTS

8. Do not use a dictionary in the exam to look up words which were not included in your prepared essay

READING & LISTENING EXAMS

9. You will not understand every word, but you don't need to
10. Know how to manipulate information in the text
11. Answer the question in the right language and tense
12. Give the information you are asked to give

VOCABULARY

13. Learn it in small chunks, but regularly
14. Come up with ways of remembering words
15. Revise vocab

GRAMMAR

16. Don't forget grammar
17. It is not necessary to write down or say the person you are using
18. Learn *haber*
19. Don't get noun genders wrong if you are given them

Your Notes

Books in this Series

Follow Us Online

Discover loads of useful resources and find out about all of our current and future products by joining the Exam Grade Booster community online.

Visit us: www.examgradebooster.co.uk

Follow us: @ExamGradeBoost

Watch us: Exam Grade Booster

Like us: Exam Grade Booster

+1 us: Exam Grade Booster

Write For Us

| Want to become an author yourself? | Want to earn money? | Want to have something hugely impressive on your UCAS form or CV? |

Go to **www.examgradebooster.co.uk** and find the **Write for Us** page. This page should have all the information you are after, but if you have any other questions you can contact us via the website. In order to write for us, you will have to complete a very straight-forward application process (there is a short form to fill out at the bottom of the *Write for Us* page). Should you be deemed suitable to write a book, you will be given access to all of our manuscripts, formatting, cover design and branding as well as having the immediate advantage of working with people, just like yourself, who have succeeded in writing their very own books.

Do it:

- Alone
  ... It is possible; I wrote *Exam Grade Booster: GCSE French* while I was still at school.
- With your friends
  ... We have a number of books being written by groups of friends to lighten the work load.

Exam Grade Booster

Lightning Source UK Ltd.
Milton Keynes UK
UKHW050924131118
332196UK00004B/52/P